JESUS AND THE GOSPEL OF GOD

JESUS
AND THE GOSPEL
OF GOD

by

DON CUPITT

Dean of Emmanuel College, Cambridge

LUTTERWORTH PRESS
GUILDFORD AND LONDON

First published 1979

For Sally

ISBN 0 7188 2397 4

*Filmset in 11/12 point Bembo
Printed and bound in Great Britain
by W & J Mackay Limited, Chatham*

CONTENTS

PREFACE: THE RETURN OF THE OLD RELIGION   7

1. THE INCARNATION
   The Orthodox Doctrine   11
   The Weakness of Orthodoxy   13
   Dogma Dethroned   21

2. FIVE KEY IDEAS
   Dogma   24
   Criticism   28
   Myth   33
   Eschatology   36
   Faith   41

3. JESUS THE TEACHER
   The Kingdom of God   44
   How God Is Shown   57
   The Message and the Messenger   67

4. GOD
   God the Saviour   76
   God Transcendent   82
   The Way to God   87

WORKING NOTES   95

INDEX   101

PREFACE: THE RETURN OF THE OLD RELIGION

When in the nineteenth century standards of critical scholarship began to rise, and the gospels were read with a better knowledge of their Jewish background, it quickly emerged that the historical Jesus had been decidedly different from the orthodox church view of him. Even today most people find this point very hard to grasp, but it is the explanation of the extraordinary twists and turns (and the consequent bad reputation) of modern theology. The customary picture of Jesus as having been consciously God incarnate on earth, wielding divine powers and teaching the Christian view of himself, his status and his task, was found to be incorrect. It was so severely distorted that it would be better to abandon it entirely and start again.

Christianity has instead to be seen as a religion that gradually evolved through a whole series of major transformations: from Jesus to the apostolic church, to the ancient church, and finally to the conciliar orthodoxy of Christendom. As with an ancient building that has been repeatedly modified, traces of the earlier stages of its history remained after each transformation. But eventually the faith evolved so far away from Jesus as to be incompatible with his original message and outlook. Those whose primary allegiance was to the developed dogmas could not stretch far enough back to do justice to Jesus. Those who started with Jesus could not reach far enough forward to be able to stomach the developed dogmas.

The single most illuminating distinction for understanding Christianity is that between the primitive *eschatological* faith and the developed *dogmatic* faith.

The primitive faith was at its purest in the teaching of the Baptist, Jesus, and the first generation of Jesus' followers. It was intensely practical and immediate, concerned only with

7

the coming of God and the gaining of salvation, and richly metaphorical in its language. But after the mid-50's or thereabouts it began to be thought that the risen Jesus was not merely waiting briefly in the wings but was semi-permanently enthroned in heaven, and the long slow transformation of the primitive faith into the developed faith began.

For the primitive faith Jesus was not God incarnate. There was no way of saying such a thing, nor was it necessary to say it. Jesus was simply experienced as Messiah, Saviour, Lord, and Son of God (which was *not* a divine title). He was imaginatively and mythologically connected with a whole host of heavenly beings and powers—dead prophets, angels, heavenly redeemer-figures and divine attributes. But he could not be simply identified with God the Father, and there was no available notion of a distinction of co-equal persons within the one God. Thus the idea of the incarnation simply could not be stated within the available thought-forms, even if the early Christians had wished to state it. Indeed, for two centuries Christian language was quite vague and imprecise, and there is much to be said for the view that the idea of the incarnation of God in Jesus did not properly speaking exist until the concept of a distinction of equal persons within God had been clearly formulated, and that only occurred in about the third century. Before that time we cannot be sure that we are not reading back later ideas into the texts.

The developed dogmatic faith is essentially an adaptation of Christianity to the requirements of Greco-Roman culture, and especially to the demands of establishment. Every ancient society was based on a cosmology, and political and religious authority descended from the gods. There was a great concern with cosmic rank, correct belief, authority and obedience. The church of Jesus the Messiah found itself in the business of creating a picture of the cosmic order, defining its place in history and becoming the basis of a civilization. The old eschatological faith had nothing to do with any of these things, and was largely discarded. But the new Christendom-Christianity naturally claimed to be a valid interpretation of the New Testament, and read back its dogmas into the original metaphors. To this day most people retain a deeply-engrained habit of reading Christendom's dogmas into the New Testa-

8

ment, and many theologians still struggle to reconcile the New Testament with developed Christianity.

It cannot go on. Today the balance of the argument has swung irreversibly against the developed dogmatic faith. The social order and the cosmology it created have passed away, its historical foundations have crumbled, and it cannot be defended either as an exegesis of the New Testament or for the way it uses Jesus' name. It is necessary now to abandon the remains of Christendom habits of thinking, and to start again from Jesus himself. I believe the primitive faith is intelligible and defensible where Christendom is not, and that the stock objections that we know too little of Jesus, and that what we do know is too strange to be intelligible today, can be overcome. The old religion is returning. Christianity's first task today is the restoration of its own integrity. It must eject Constantine, give up the old craving for power, and become a pure religion of salvation again.

Luther reshaped Christianity around Paul's doctrine of justification by faith. He started from Paul, not from Jesus, and did not penetrate deeply enough into Jesus' own ways of speaking. He recovered some elements of Christianity, and affirmed them with an eloquence and force that has never been equalled. But he still wanted Christianity to remain an instrument of social control, and the older Lutheran Churches are established churches. This prevented him from recognizing that primitive Christianity was overwhelmingly eschatological in its concerns. The early Christians themselves had explained their faith by beginning with the preaching of the Baptist and Jesus, but Luther began with Paul and bequeathed to theologians the habit of doing the same, and he still read Christendom dogmas back into the New Testament.

So today a reformation more thorough than Luther's is called for: there is no other way of restoring the real Jesus to his proper centrality in Christian faith. The false cult of Jesus as a human god must go, so that the words of the real Jesus can be heard again. Above all we must find some way of taking into our souls and rediscovering the inwardness of the primitive Christian eschatology.

The programme I am setting out could scarcely be more demanding. I hope this little book is pointing in the right

9

general direction, but cannot claim more than that for it. In chapter 1, I take the central doctrine of the developed faith, the incarnation, and try to show how the arguments for it have broken down. In chapter 2, the change of orientation required is explored by examining five key concepts. In chapters 3 and 4, I search for the religious meaning of Jesus' message and its implications for belief in God.

Many people will see all this as a piece of shallow demythologizing, peeling the onion when what I ought to be doing is defending the metaphysical presuppositions of the developed faith, and decoding its complex mythical structure. For them it is the developed faith that counts, and I am being tiresomely reductionist.

I do not agree. The developed faith locked Christianity into a particular cultural and political tradition which lasted more or less till the Enlightenment, and was revived after a fashion in the nineteenth century, but has now passed away. It was always a severe distortion of the original faith. In trying to go back behind it, behind the superstructure of dogma and philosophy to the initial, purely religious impulse at the core, I believe I can see something more universal and more powerful.

But what is it? The purely religious cannot be said plainly, only shown, and those who have the power to show it are very rare indeed. But it is the pearl of great price, in comparison with which everything else is worthless. It is necessary to be uncompromising in the search for it.

1

THE INCARNATION

In most people's minds the essential and distinctive feature of Christianity is its belief in the divinity of Jesus Christ. Those who believe that Jesus is God are Christians and those who do not believe it are not, so that when Christian theologians question the divinity of Christ there is general bewilderment and some indignation. Accordingly we must begin by setting out some of the reasons for the doubts, for no one is going to be much interested in the construction of an alternative account of the meaning of Jesus unless he is first persuaded that the old account is indefensible.

The Orthodox Doctrine

The first task—not an easy one—is to say just what is meant by the belief in the divinity of Jesus. The doctrine to which the mainstream of Christianity is committed was defined in stages and through bitter controversies between the Council of Nicaea (AD 325) and the Council of Chalcedon (AD 451).

The full Chalcedonian definition incorporates two creeds, three letters and a complex statement about the nature of Jesus Christ. It is highly technical, but the gist of it is that the Lord Jesus Christ is truly, completely, and perfectly both divine and human. As God the Father's divine Son he is co-essential and co-eternal with the Father. That is, he is eternally everything that God is in the way that God is, save only that the Father is the Father and he is the Son. And as the son of Mary the Virgin Mother of God he is human, born in time. His two natures, divine and human, are permanently united without confusion, division or separation. He is 'God from everlasting, man for evermore'. The subject who lived the life of Jesus on earth was the second person of the Trinity in the fullness of his divine being, yet that life was also a human life and Jesus had a human body and a human rational soul.

The Council ends by declaring that this is the teaching of the prophets, of Jesus himself, and of the church. Converts to Christianity may not be taught anything else.

Much is obscure in all this, but at least it is clear that when Christians say Jesus is God they do not mean that Jesus is numerically identical with God the Father, nor that Jesus is the only divine being worshipped by them. Nor do they worship three Gods, for the Father, the Son and the Holy Spirit are said to be one God in three persons. But they are saying that Jesus was and is a being co-equal and co-eternal with God. The express intention of the Council of Nicea was to rule out any subordination of Jesus to God and to declare him equal in rank with God the Father.

In a few words, then, mainstream Christian believers hold that Jesus of Nazareth, God's incarnate Son, was everything that God is in the way that God is, save only that the Father is the Father and the Son is the Son. Jesus is, as the Nicene creed says, 'of one substance with the Father,' (the Greek word is *homoousios*).

This doctrine was only defined in the fourth and fifth centuries, in the period when Christianity was settling down as the official state religion of the later Roman Empire. Before that time there was more latitude of opinion. The change can be illustrated by comparing the Apostles' creed with the Nicene creed.

The Apostles' creed has a long and obscure history which need not concern us here. Suffice it to say that it belongs to the western church, is of ultimately pre-Nicene origin, and is in the main couched in the language of the New Testament. Believers profess their faith 'in Jesus Christ his only Son our Lord'. This gives Jesus three titles: Christ (or Messiah), Lord, and God's only Son. The meaning is that Jesus has in the providence of God brought in the age of universal salvation (Christ), that he lives and reigns over this new age (Lord), and that he and he alone is God's plenipotentiary, the one appointed to be God's viceroy or representative (the only Son of God).

These three titles—Lord, Christ and only Son of God—strongly emphasize the centrality of Jesus in the Christian scheme of salvation and are already in the New Testament regarded as the distinctively Christian titles. But they leave the question of Jesus' metaphysical status quite open. His 'person' might be that of a man, a heavenly being, a subordinate divine being or a co-equal divine being. The titles are compatible with any of those four views. All that matters is that Jesus is pre-eminently the one through whom God gives eternal salvation.

In the Nicene creed the options are closed. This creed also has a complicated history, but the form of words laid down in 325 required that the phrase 'Son of God' be henceforth understood not just in its traditional functional and 'economic' sense but in an ontological or 'essential' sense. Jesus was declared to be God's eternally begotten and co-equally divine Son: he is 'the Son of God, begotten from the Father, only-begotten, that is, from the substance of the Father, God from God, light from light, true God from true God, begotten not made, of one substance with the Father'.

Since 325, then, mainstream Christian belief has been that the one who lived the life of Jesus was in the fullest sense God, co-equal and co-eternal with God the Father. Defenders of Nicene orthodoxy do not, of course, admit that their faith came into existence in 325. They claim that Nicaea merely made more explicit what had been the implicit faith of the church from the very first. My view is that the Apostles' creed form of words is defensible, because it is in accord with reason and Christian experience, with the New Testament evidence, and with the life and message of Jesus. But the Nicene creed's form of words is not defensible, for a whole range of reasons. So I am bound to scrutinize closely the arguments put forward by the defenders of Nicaea.

The Weakness of Orthodoxy

Since the rise of the modern view of history it has come to be accepted that everything in our historical knowledge is relative and merely probable, and nothing is certain. But if so, it is

13

very hard to see how there can be an argument which begins with historical statements and concludes that something absolute and more-than-historical has entered history. What sort of evidence could there be which could oblige us to admit that a certain historical figure though in every observable respect human was really more than human—was even co-equal with God? How could mere historical evidence with all its uncertainties ever justify such a stupendous affirmation?

Some people are tempted to say that of course the incarnation cannot be proved; it must simply be believed. But this will not explain how the doctrine arose in the first place, for those who framed it and made it binding upon the church certainly thought there was a case for it. They produced arguments, and arguments are still being produced today. How strong are they?

Many of the traditional arguments, like the arguments from prophecy and from miracles, are very weak. The mere fact that *prophecies are fulfilled in Jesus* no more proves him divine than the fact that prophecies are fulfilled in John the Baptist proves the Baptist divine. It may be replied that Jesus fulfils messianic prophecies, but the Messiah is not in the Bible a co-equal divine being. On the contrary he is a human figure, though he may here and there be regarded as a created pre-existent heavenly being.

The *argument from miracles* states that Jesus performed miracles, works such as only God can do, and that Jesus is therefore God. But virtually all the miracle stories associated with Jesus can be paralleled elsewhere in the Bible and Jewish tradition, and nobody has ever argued that Elishah and others were divine beings. Therefore quite apart from historical-critical questions the argument from Jesus' miracles is invalid. Moreover Jesus' *resurrection* is not in the New Testament a unique event that proves his divinity, but the beginning of a general resurrection in which every baptized believer already participates.

Appeal is sometimes made to the *moral splendour of Jesus' teaching*. But there seems no reason why God should not communicate perfect moral teaching through a man. After all, Jews and Muslims believe that just this has happened. So again we need not raise critical questions about whether Jesus' teach-

14

ing is in fact perfect or how we could judge it to be so, for the argument is in any case unsound.

Some argue from *Jesus' sinlessness*. But apart from the fact that we do not have and perhaps never could have enough evidence, there is the often-overlooked point that one of the best-attested facts about Jesus' life is that he voluntarily underwent a baptism of repentance.

Others appeal to *Jesus' authority* and the assurance with which, in his reported sayings, he overrides or amends traditional religious teaching. The immediacy, freedom and power of his teaching is of course not in dispute, but it can scarcely be sufficient to show his co-equal divinity.

The same goes for his alleged *claims* and for the famous *trilemma argument*, which asserts that one who makes such claims must be either a madman, an imposter, or genuine; but we cannot think him to be a madman or an imposter, so we must accept his claims.

The first difficulty here is to pin down the claims. The upshot of modern study of the gospels is that they have largely evaporated. There is no reliable evidence that Jesus claimed co-equal divinity. He did not publicly proclaim his Messiahship and even his use of the term Son of Man is not free from ambiguity, for he seems sometimes to have spoken of the Son of Man as a figure distinct from himself. That he considered himself to have a special mission from God cannot be doubted, but he is strikingly evasive about his own precise status. The title 'Son of God' in biblical usage is ordinarily a human title. A close filial communion with God, dependence upon God and obedience to God is an ideal for all believers, so it by no means follows that one who has an intense filial awareness of God must himself be co-equal with God.

The point is that we should be careful about moving from an exalted mystical sense of unity with God to metaphysical equality with God. The Islamic mystic al-Hallaj, probably influenced by the Jesus of John's gospel, declared *ana'l-haqq*, 'I am the Truth' and was crucified for blasphemy in AD 922, because al-Haqq, the Truth, is one of the names of God in the Qur'an. The weakness and clumsiness of the trilemma argument is apparent if we apply it to his case. There is no reason to think him mad or bad, but nor does anyone claim that he must

15

therefore be a unique incarnation of God. Al-Hallaj, like many other mystics, was testifying to an exalted state of union with God. Thus Jesus' awareness of God, even supposing that we could discover its quality by historical enquiry, would not by itself do anything to prove him a co-equal divine being.

The arguments about Jesus' claims raise a crucial point, one so important that the case deserves to be set out formally:

1. Christianity is a monotheistic faith.
2. In monotheism it is of the essence of the idea of God that God is 'living', pure intelligent Spirit.
3. A being that is God knows it is God. There cannot be in monotheism a slumbering or unconscious deity.
4. So if Jesus were God incarnate, then Jesus knew that he was God incarnate.
5. But there is no reliable empirical evidence that Jesus thought he was a co-equal divine person or claimed to be such, and there is a great deal of evidence to the contrary.
6. Therefore there is no case for the incarnation and a strong case against it.

This argument has been understood for a long time, and the various theories of Christ which postulate some putting-off of divine attributes and veiling of divine consciousness are attempts to overcome the difficulty. But they cannot succeed without either falling into a corrupt idea of God (that God can be scaled down to human level and even become unconscious, and yet remain God), or separating the doctrine from the man Jesus. In that case it is no longer said that there is a self-revelation of God *in* Jesus, but that the incarnation doctrine is something God has revealed *about* Jesus. The full meaning of the doctrine of the incarnation is then lost, and something rather different is said instead. This has already happened, but people have been slow to admit it.

Another argument starts from *Jesus' exercise of divine functions* such as forgiveness, judgment and salvation. One who exercises divine powers such as these must, it is claimed, be himself divine. This is not so, for the ordinary biblical view is that God may act through a human agent to forgive, judge and save. Jesus himself is portrayed as giving 'the keys of the kingdom of heaven' to his own *human* followers. When he says, 'Your sins are forgiven,' Jesus is using a construction

16

called 'the divine passive'. His meaning is not, 'I forgive you,' but, 'I assure you that God forgives you.' And there are several well-known sayings in which Jesus insists that not he but God alone is good, just and all-knowing. Similarly, to say that Jesus is Saviour is to affirm (as I do) that in Jesus God has given to men the definitive way to final salvation, but it does not follow that the one through whom salvation is given must be himself co-equal with God.

Many people claim *communion with Jesus in religious experience*. They recognize as a god one whose lineaments are those of the figure portrayed in the gospels. There is a general question here about the nature of religious experience. Psychologically it seems beyond doubt that the experient projects his own beliefs into his religious experience, so that experiences of Jesus as God are created by the belief that he is God and cannot without circularity be used as evidence in support of that belief. More generally, not all claims to be able to recognize a particular deity in religious experience can be genuine, for such claims have doubtless been made on behalf of thousands of gods. The only way forward is by evaluating such claims theologically. And there can be no doubt that the standard Christian form of prayer since New Testament times has been to God through Jesus Christ our Lord, rather than directly to Jesus. To this day standard liturgical forms remain remarkably conservative and still reflect a pre-Nicene theology. Jesus taught his disciples to pray to God as Father, and Christians pray to God the Father through Jesus, that is, in his Way. But prayer direct to Jesus as God, which has become more and more common in modern times, has moved too far away from the wholly God-centred outlook of Jesus himself to be acceptable.

It is sometimes argued that in the New Testament *prayer to Jesus* occurs; but in a Jewish milieu only God could be prayed to, so prayer to Jesus implies belief that Jesus is God. Prayer to Jesus was in fact very rare in early times, but in any case the argument is unsound, for as the New Testament itself reminds us it was possible at that time to pray to a figure like Elijah who was seen as eschatological deliverer.

A more general question is that of *whether the New Testament teaches the co-equal divinity of Jesus*. We may well ask in what

17

sense the New Testament teaches anything, because it is a collection of books in which many very different things are said or implied by the various authors and by the characters within their books. But in view of the fact that the incarnation of God in Jesus is supposed to be the distinctive Christian belief, it is very striking that it should be so hard to say whether the idea is really taught in the New Testament at all.

The issue is so complex that I can only give the briefest impression of what was held by Jesus, the synoptic gospel-writers, Paul and John. Jesus did not claim to be God. The author of Luke-Acts does not claim that Jesus is God. Matthew and Mark may possibly have ascribed some kind of heavenly or subordinate divine status to Jesus, but that is not the same as co-equal divinity. Paul sees Christ as pre-existent and as presently enthroned as God's 'Son' or executive, but unlike later theology he firmly subordinates Jesus Christ to God the Father. Among this group of basic New Testament teachers John alone calls Jesus 'God' or perhaps 'divine'. But he appears to mean that Jesus is the perfect expression or revelation of God, and like the rest of the New Testament writers he is also careful to affirm that God the Father is the only God (e.g. John 5:44, 17:3) and is the God of Jesus (e.g. 20:17).

In conclusion, in so far as it is possible to summarize the teaching of the New Testament, it is this: the way to God opened up by Jesus, and the salvation offered through him, are perfect and final. He is exalted to God's right hand as Lord, Christ and Son of God. He *is* God's revelation. But the New Testament remains monotheistic. God the Father is the only God, and the early Christians were most reluctant to name Jesus God absolutely. The New Testament does not teach the later standard doctrine that Jesus is a distinct divine person co-equal, co-essential and co-eternal with God the Father. It exalts Jesus as high as is possible without compromising monotheism.

An excellent example of just what the New Testament says occurs at 1 Corinthians 8:6. Because it is so early in date, and exalts Jesus so high, it is often cited as evidence for his divinity. However the precise form of words shows not Jesus' divinity, but the continuing restraining influence of Paul's Jewish monotheism: 'There is one God, the Father, from whom all being comes, towards whom we move; and there is one Lord, Jesus Christ, through whom all things came to be, and we through him.' (New English Bible translation: this text is cited *for* the divinity of Christ by the orthodox, and *against* it by the Jehovah's Witnesses!)

It is difficult to press the New Testament further than that without forcing the exegesis. Many writers do it, by exploiting the range of possible meanings of terms like 'Lord' or 'worship', but the very fact of the need to go to such lengths is evidence of the weakness of the case.

One example comes in the Letter to the Hebrews where God is depicted as saying to the Son (i.e. Jesus Christ), 'Thy throne, O God, is for ever and ever,' (1:8). If God the Father calls Jesus God, then surely he is God. But the line has an Old Testament background in Psalm 45:6, where it refers to the king of Israel, and Isaiah 9:6, where the messianic king is addressed as 'mighty God'. No exegete would suggest that the Hebrew writers thought of either their present king or their ideal future king as literally and co-equally divine. As the alternative possible translations 'God is thy throne . . .' or 'Thy throne, like God, . . .' suggest, the meaning is rather that the king rules by divine right and is endued with the fullness of God's power. The writer to the Hebrews sees Jesus as fulfilling all the expectations of Israelite faith. Mythologically, he exalts Jesus in the cosmos to God's right hand and declares Jesus to be God's revelation in his own person: but he does not take the further step of declaring Jesus a second divine person co-equal with God the Father. He stays with Paul and John.

I conclude that the true New Testament teaching is preserved in the Apostle's creed, and that the Nicene creed goes a crucial step beyond anything the New Testament says. From the early second century some writers, such as Ignatius of Antioch, did begin to speak baldly of Jesus as God absolutely and as in effect a 'second God' alongside God the Father. But the New Testament does not support such language. And in the New Testament generally the mark of a Christian is not that he believes that Jesus is God but that he believes Jesus is Lord, Messiah and Son of God.

In passing, it is particularly important to be fully aware of the ambiguities of the phrase 'Son of God'. When he was

19

condemning the 'errors of the modernists' in the encyclical *Lamentabili* of the 3rd July 1907 Pope Pius X condemned the following proposition: 'In all the evangelical texts the name "Son of God" is equivalent only to that of "Messias". It does not in the least way signify that Christ is the true and natural Son of God.' The Pope asserts by implication that the true Christian doctrine is that Jesus *is* the true and natural Son of God. But the unqualified use of the phrase 'true and natural' appears to assimilate the Christian doctrine to the theogonies of pagan religion, and is quite incompatible with true monotheism. It is mythological, a myth being a story depicting one or more deities as having human traits, behaving in human ways and so on. Religious language is mythological when it portrays the deity as subject to human emotions, as begetting offspring, as descending from heaven to earth and later returning to heaven, and as acting with motives like human motives. But God is not human, and strictly speaking monotheistic faith ought to aim at being quite myth-free. Some mythological elements must always remain while God is spoken of in human language, but we must be constantly on our guard against being misled by them.

The deepest appeal of the doctrine of the incarnation is its appeal to our human need for a god who is human. 'I must believe,' people say, 'in a God who cares enough to involve himself, to share our sorrows, to stand alongside us and to suffer our fate.' Yet this demand runs embarrassingly close to what the prophets would have called a pagan lust after idolatry. Terrified of the true God, we turn aside and seek instead a friendly human god. But the true God who is changelessly transcendent, whose name and action cannot properly be described, but who yet gives the Spirit, salvation and forgiveness, and who is incomprehensibly close and gracious, was enough for Jesus and ought to be enough for his followers.

So there are strong reasons for doubting whether the doctrine of the co-equal divinity of Jesus really is the essence of Christianity. I claim that it does not accurately represent the message of the New Testament as a whole, and that it is so foreign to the message and outlook of Jesus himself that where it is believed the teaching of the real Jesus tends to be forgotten. We can already see this happening in the New Testament, for in the New Testament books the higher the doctrinal claims made about Jesus become, the more the historical reality of the man and his message are obscured.

The classic example of this process is John's gospel. John certainly approaches the full doctrine of the incarnation, for he regards Jesus as being in his own person God's revelation incarnate. But he can only represent Jesus thus by transforming his message so much that the original man is barely recognizable. At a later stage still, in the documents of the Council of Chalcedon the outlook and values of Jesus himself have been almost wholly buried. The Christ of developed dogma takes over, and Jesus becomes no more than a point of contact between the Christ of dogma and history. Thomas Corbishley, a recent Jesuit writer, has put it, 'We are . . . committed to the view that the Risen Christ, a cosmic figure, reconciling the world, restoring all things, is immensely more significant than anything explicitly stated in the words of the itinerant preacher, living under the Emperor Tiberius and the governor Pilate.' (*The Prayer of Jesus*, A. R. Mowbray 1976, page 10.)

What this author sees as a matter of pride, I regard as a revealing admission. Christianity quickly evolved so far away from the outlook and values of Jesus that it has been scarcely justified in using his name at all. Only recently have books about the doctrine of Christ begun to pay attention to the real Jesus, as his message has begun to be better understood. And the more seriously we take his message the more impatient we shall become with many of the classical doctrines about him.

Dogma Dethroned

All the mainstream Christian churches teach, as Chalcedon taught, that the full orthodox doctrine of the incarnation is the teaching of scripture and can be proved from scripture. But closer examination has shown us how uncertain the connection between scripture and orthodox doctrine really is. We took one example, the incarnation, but we would have reached similar conclusions if we had taken other major doctrines of the church, such as the distinct personality of the Holy Spirit, the co-existence therefore of three persons in the one God, and

21

so on. It has become clear how curiously ramshackle and loosely connected with scripture the whole system of traditional doctrine is; so much so that by now study of the teachings of the various biblical writers has become a different literary *genre* from dogmatic theology, which is left hanging in the air.

How can traditional Christian doctrine be defended if its New Testament basis is doubtful? On the usual view, there occurred a revelation from God at the beginning of Christianity which the New Testament preserves. Christian doctrine, it is claimed, is taught in the New Testament; or implied in the New Testament; or is a legitimate 'development' of what is taught in the New Testament; or is consistent, or at any rate not inconsistent, with what is taught in the New Testament. The more cautious phrases here invite us to ask just how far the church can go beyond the New Testament. If Christian doctrine extrapolates, turning into a system what is unsystematic in the sources, and ruling out interpretations which are not ruled out in the sources, at what point does serious distortion begin to occur?

These are old questions. They became of vital importance when Protestantism challenged the way the doctrines of the Roman Catholic Church had been developing since very early times. Classical Christianity had assumed the unity of scripture and tradition, and while that was assumed it was impossible to question the process of development. People then did not have our sort of historical consciousness. They took it absolutely for granted that Jesus, Paul, and the contemporary church were all unanimous. But once a real historical development of doctrine was admitted things could never be the same again. The Protestants might like to pretend that the New Testament taught a single faith, and that the New Testament faith was identical with the faith they themselves professed. But in the end they could not help recognizing doctrinal differences within the New Testament itself, and between the New Testament and their own doctrines. Today we have to admit that the age of religious innocence is over. Once we understand biblical criticism and the human, historically conditioned character of religious ideas, our viewpoint must change. As D. F. Strauss said, 'The true criticism of

22

dogma is its history.' (Cited by Peter C. Hodgson in his introduction to D. F. Strauss, *The Life of Jesus Critically Examined*, translated by George Eliot 1846, re-issued S.C.M. Press, 1973, page xlv.) It is impossible to maintain that Christianity is now and always has been a single clear, distinct and unchangeable set of beliefs.

To see this is to realize that the age of dogmatic Christianity is ending and that we are moving into a new era. The change of outlook that is called for is very considerable. It is not a shift from conservative definiteness to liberal woolliness, but a shift from dogmatic to critical faith. Going back behind the dogmatic superstructure in search of the meaning of Jesus, critical faith picks out three ancient and vital themes: the pure prophetic faith that God is one and God is Spirit, the message of Jesus, and the eschatological faith of the first Christians. Each of these themes was obscured and partly lost in the developed dogmatic faith and each needs to be rediscovered and re-affirmed.

2

FIVE KEY IDEAS

The best way to introduce the change of outlook that I am
describing is through short analyses of five key ideas: dogma,
criticism, myth, eschatology, and faith.

Dogma

Christianity was not at first dogmatic. Jesus was not at all a
dogmatic instructor, and the writings of his early followers are
not in the later sense works of 'dogmatic theology'. In the
New Testament the word dogma appears only in the non-
technical sense of a decree issued by some authority, and the
earliest Christians did not have creeds. It was sufficient for
them to distinguish themselves from other Jews by slogans
such as 'Jesus is Lord', 'the Messiah is Jesus', and brief summaries (such as 1 Corinthians 15:3ff.) of their claims about the
fulfilment of scripture in Jesus. What distinguishes a Jew is not
the profession of a creed but membership of a community that
lives by a certain sacred Law, and similarly the first Christians
saw themselves as following the Way or the Law of Christ.

In the latest New Testament books the beginnings of a set
'pattern of sound doctrine' taught to converts can be made out.
In the Gentile world such a set of teachings might be called
dogmas, just as the teachings of the various philosophical sects
might be called dogmas.

The standard Christian sense of 'dogma' comes a good deal
later. A dogma is a religious truth established by divine revelation, defined by the church and binding on all members of the
church. It is a truth 'above reason' which cannot be discovered
by the individual for himself by rational enquiry, but must be
received and believed upon authority. So for there to be dog-

24

mas there must be a person or body within the church with God-given authority to expound and define the Faith entrusted to the church. Christianity is coming to be thought of as *the Faith*, the teaching of the church; and saving faith, the disposition by which a person enters upon a right relation to God, is coming to be identified with orthodox belief and acceptance of church teaching. In short, for there to be dogma in this strong sense there must be the fully-developed established church, with its strongly hierarchical organization, its General Councils of Bishops, and its definitions of the Faith, without which there is no salvation.

The crucial point here is that dogmas are saving truths: one must believe them to be saved, and believe them in submission to the teaching authority of the church in general and the hierarchy in particular. The incarnation locked these ideas together, for Christ was believed to have founded the church and given it divine authority. Through the incarnation the church's authority was no less than God's.

It is just this kind of Christianity which is dying today, overwhelmed by historical criticism, by individualistic and libertarian ways of thinking, and by awareness of religious diversity. Its more extravagant manifestations can attract ridicule, as when the 'Athanasian creed' asserts that one will perish everlastingly unless one steadfastly adheres to an exceedingly technical definition of the Trinity and the incarnation. But its influence remains very strong, nevertheless. It is shown in the widespread feeling that if the doctrine of the incarnation be denied nothing is left of Christianity, and in the claim that one who denies some part of 'the teaching of the church' ought not to remain in the church.

Thus it is worth recalling that Christianity was not at first dogmatic, but only became so under certain pressures of a political kind. The New Testament does not teach 'the Faith' in the same sense as the church has taught 'the Faith' since the fourth century. Today even the most orthodox scholars admit that many doctrines which orthodoxy regards as essential to salvation cannot easily be 'proved' from scripture.

Protestants recognized that the progressive definition of dogma was alien to the spirit of the New Testament and had gone well beyond what the New Testament could conceivably justify. So they taught that scripture alone was sufficient for salvation. But they could not wholly shake off the dogmatic habit, for they themselves produced 'confessions', summaries of what they believed to be the doctrines taught by scripture.

A few Protestants were anti-dogmatic. When William Chillingworth declared that 'the Bible and the Bible alone is the religion of Protestants' he was opposing dogmatism of the Calvinist type. He was saying that saving faith is practical and experimental, and one really ought to confine oneself to speaking as scripture does, and not erect a dogmatic superstructure upon scripture.

But even this position, though it marks a great improvement upon Roman Catholic and Protestant dogmatism, still contains a paradox. It sets up a Christian book-religion resembling other forms of book-religion, but it cannot conceal the fact that the book itself contains a triumphant cry that 'scripture is fulfilled', the age of book-religion is over, and the long-awaited time of religious immediacy and perfection has begun. Jesus and his early followers acted in the belief that the direct reign of God was beginning, the Spirit was poured out, and believers were already endowed in an anticipatory way with the powers of the new era.

The defender of book-religion has to explain how Christianity can have subsequently regressed from that original immediacy and finality. The explanation he offers is that there are three ages of religion. The first is that of the primary revelation, the age of miracles, prophecy and direct inspiration which in the case of Christianity runs from John the Baptist to the moment when the last apostolic writer laid down his pen. The second age is the age of the book. No fresh revelation can occur within this interim period, and though there are many charismatic and revivalist movements there is deep suspicion when they attempt to move outside the received framework. Enthusiasm must be kept within bounds. The divine Spirit still inspires and instructs believers, but does so within fixed limits. Faith is mediated and limited by scripture. But this state of affairs is transitional, for in the future or the beyond religious immediacy will return in the third and final age of faith.

This account gives Christian book-religion the same structure as Jewish book-religion. Even before Jesus' time the Jews also distinguished three ages. During the age of Moses and the prophets God spoke directly to his people, but then the Spirit was quenched, and in the long waiting-period which followed only the 'echo' of God's voice was heard. People remembered, studied, wrote commentaries, and waited in hope. But eventually the Spirit would return, the Messiah would come, and a final glorious age of religious spontaneity and immediacy would begin.

It is curious that in spite of its belief that the Messiah has already come, historical Christianity should have ended with the same logical structure as Jewish religion, rather as if the only difference between Christianity and Judaism is that the former is catholic and the latter ethnic. The claim that the Messiah has actually come seems to have got lost.

This analysis points to the true meaning of Orthodox, Catholic and Protestant dogmatism. Albert Schweitzer used to say that the entire history of what we call 'Christianity' is based upon the non-occurrence or delay of the parousia, the final 'coming' of God. Jesus and the first generation of his followers lived in a condition of eschatological joy and ardent expectation of the speedy consummation of the kingdom of God. Christian theology began as a representation of how things stood in the brief interval between the death and resurrection of Jesus and the final victory of God. But gradually the flame began to die down and the historical perspective ahead began to look longer and longer. Eschatological and immediate faith slowly developed into historical and dogmatic faith. Jesus was not just briefly waiting in heaven, but permanently enthroned there. The immediate enjoyment of final blessedness was exchanged for a dogmatic guarantee that those who believed the church's faith and were sacramentally united with Jesus were entitled to hope for a favourable verdict at the Last Assize.

Dogmatic faith, then, is historical in two senses. It was through a process of historical development that faith came to take this form; but still more important, dogmatic faith is a framework of ideas evolved precisely to enable believers to endure the continuation of history. It is often said that Christianity is an historical religion, but it was originally a very

27

strongly eschatological faith. Although there is no evidence that at some moment the original hope was dismissed as being factually mistaken, we can say that it gradually faded and historical-dogmatic faith, a this-worldly cosmology and system of social control based on the incarnation, came to replace it.

So it would be more accurate to reverse the stock phrase and speak not of the Jesus of history and the Christ of faith but of the Jesus of faith and the dogmatic Christ of history. The dogmatic Christ, the God-man born in time, dying a sacrificial death for the sins of all mankind and ascending to heaven to sit at God's right hand, authorizing the church and guaranteeing its sacraments, is a product of history. Through the long centuries of Christendom he assured believers that the absolute and final had touched human life, and if they held fast to him they would in the end be saved. To this day the dogmatic theologian attempts to re-word and reinforce that solemn guarantee. But it is still a second-best. The original Jesus is the greater figure, just as the kingdom is a higher category than the church, eschatology surpasses history, and immediate faith surpasses mediated faith.

So when I set aside the dogma of the incarnation I do so in order to point to something greater; for, I repeat, the human Jesus, the harbinger of the kingdom of God, is a qualitatively greater figure than the divine Christ of church history. The problem of Christian renewal today is, as always, to see how something of Christianity's original finality can be recaptured. How can we transcend the outworn historical-dogmatic faith of the church and regain something of the pure faith of the kingdom of God?

Criticism

Being inclined to expect the worst, people often use the word criticism to mean adverse criticism, just as they use conscience in the sense of guilty conscience. Yet criticism properly understood means no more than exact and careful appraisal. The critical method and outlook are in the humanities what the scientific method and outlook are in the study of nature, and though it is often said that it is natural science which has over the past few centuries done the most to undermine traditional religious belief, it is arguable that the critical historical method has done even more.

Nowadays terms like 'criticism', 'critical' and 'critique' are used in a great variety of senses (and often in a rather uncritical way), but we can pick out a central cluster of ideas.

The word criticism has been used since the Renaissance to mean careful and unprejudiced assessment, comparison and judgement. In this sense critical scholarship is merely good scholarship, and as such nothing new. But a certain degree of self-awareness is called for even at this simple level, for a judge hearing evidence needs criteria for deciding rationally what may count as evidence, what is the status of a witness, and how to deal with conflicting evidence. As critical thinker, a judge in a law court is not so purely objective that his mind is a total blank. On the contrary, he must be acutely aware of the rational principles in terms of which he weighs the evidence as he hears it.

We can take this same example a stage further. An experienced judge, who has sat on the Bench for many years and has thought long about evidence he has heard and the principles by which he has learnt to weigh it, will come to two conclusions. First, no evidence at all can be accepted dogmatically as certainly trustworthy and incorrigible. Even what seems to be the most reliable and first-hand testimony may need to be reappraised in the light of something else that is said later. But secondly, there is no reason for outright scepticism. Courts are not infallible, but nor are they worthless. Laborious, imperfect and provisional though it is, court procedure is a way of arriving at truth which in practice works pretty well, and if fresh evidence should subsequently turn up, or if it should become evident that the earlier evidence was grossly misinterpreted, then the case can be heard again.

This example helps to make clear a number of points made by the philosopher Immanuel Kant (1724–1804), who did so much to shape the modern uses of the term 'critical'. Criticism is not just careful judgement, for it must also be judgement in which we are critically aware of the principles upon which we judge. Kant defined *Kritik* as 'a science of the mere examination of pure reason, of its sources and limits' (in *Immanuel Kant's Critique of Pure Reason*, translated by Norman Kemp Smith, Macmillan 1964, page 59). For Kant, *Kritik* is a necessary defence against both the dogmatism that goes away beyond the evidence and the scepticism that denies that we can attain any knowledge at all.

Kant's idea of critique has further implications. He insisted that all our knowledge is human knowledge. Pre-critical philosophy had sought to attain a God's-eye view of reality, an absolute knowledge of things. The idea was that in the light of this absolute knowledge the lower forms of human knowledge could have assigned to them such modest degree of validity as they appeared to deserve.

Kant objected that these dogmatic metaphysicians had attempted the impossible. There is no meaning in the suggestion that I can altogether outsoar the limits of my senses and the ordinary machinery of my understanding. I can take off my sunglasses and see better without them, but I cannot take off my mind and understand better without it. We cannot validate human knowledge from outside, by placing it in relation to a system of absolute knowledge, for we cannot step outside ourselves to make the comparison. It follows that the defence of the objectivity of human knowledge has to be conducted from within, by the process of critique which we have just described. Thinking has to become critical or self-aware; it must become conscious of itself, its own workings and its own limits.

Kant was not primarily interested in history, and the influence of his ideas upon the development of the critical historical method is a further story. But the examples of court procedure and Kant's own philosophical point about human knowledge give us enough to go on for the moment. Critical thinking is profoundly anti-dogmatic. Typically, instead of starting with a dogmatically accepted theory and cramming all the facts into it, it starts from the recognition that all theories are human constructions which may account more or less well for the evidence. The progress of knowledge depends not just on the ability to pack more facts into the existing theory but still more on critical examination of theory itself, and willingness to discard it.

It may well be, as Kant himself thought, that some elements in our theory of the world are necessary, in the sense that without them we can have no objective empirical knowledge at all. But this fact is not accepted dogmatically; it is elicited by carrying out a critique. Critical thinking also recognizes that there are no theoretically-quite-neutral facts, but this is no reason for re-introducing dogmatism about theory. The lesson is rather that one must be all the more critically aware of the framework of theory in terms of which one views the evidence.

From all this it is clear that biblical criticism and historical study of the making of Christian doctrine are bound to have a dramatic effect on the way we understand religion. Religion is human, and the Bible and Christian affirmations are human historical products.

Here is just one example of the way one's point of view must change. In the New Testament and the creeds it is said that Jesus is now 'seated at the right hand of God'. I have met people who think this statement 'literally true'. Just as a foreign monarch may issue a press statement to the effect that he has appointed and installed a new Prime Minister, so God sent a dispatch—a revelation—to the apostles to inform them that Jesus had just been installed as his chief executive in heaven.

In pre-critical theology that naïve literalism was of course severely qualified. It was recognized that the phrase 'seated at God's right hand' is symbolic or metaphorical. But it was still held that the phrase, though metaphorical, had objective reference. It described clumsily what is the case in heaven and expressed a revealed truth.

But in critical theology one must go further. This phrase was invented by human beings, and we must ask if its origin and meaning can be explained on a simpler hypothesis than direct revelation from God. What experiences and what available linguistic resources might have led them to speak in this way? My tentative theory is as follows: by imaginatively and ritually identifying themselves with Jesus in his death and resurrection the apostles had come to experience a wholly new and marvellous quality of life. This they believed must be the messianic time of salvation promised in their scriptures. Jesus was therefore the Messiah. Their scriptures contain a line

31

supposedly addressed by God to the king of Israel, 'Sit at my right hand, until I make your enemies your footstool'. They applied this line to Jesus, Israel's final king. The ultimacy of the quality of life they had found in him was expressed mythologically by saying that he had ascended above all other heavenly beings to sit at God's right hand. We note that he is not displacing God, and that the mythological theme here is of great antiquity.

I have proposed an immanent historical theory of how the early Christians came to speak of Jesus as seated at the right hand of God. It is a mythological expression of a human experience, the experience of salvation. There is no need at all to think of it as describing an event in another world, or as being supernaturally communicated from heaven. The experience of salvation is in an important sense 'supernatural'; but the language in which men speak of it is human.

Religion is a human, historical product. Does it follow that critical theology must destroy not merely dogmatic religion, but all religion? Many think so, but I believe that in its own way critical thinking is profoundly religious, for it has an 'eschatological' view of truth. The thinker is conscious that his present forms of understanding are merely human, limited and provisional, and being so conscious he is always dissatisfied. This makes possible for him a present-day version of the traditional view of life as a pilgrimage towards heaven. He continually seeks clearer understanding, and is lured forward by the ideal of a complete understanding of the whole truth.

Such an ideal is unattainable in this world, because our knowledge really is human and therefore will always be limited. But the thinker cannot do without it. It motivates him, and he presupposes it all the time. He must as a matter of intellectual virtue be loyal to it, for otherwise he falters and his mind falls into the chaos of relativism and scepticism. Above all he has a kind of foretaste of it in his own intellectual freedom, that power of self-transcendence by which we can criticize ourselves, give up a habit of thought or action, and wait in receptivity for fresh illumination. It is intellectual hope, and a continual moving forward, which keeps the world a cosmos and saves it from falling into chaos.

32

The critical outlook is religious indeed, but in a new way. Dogmatic thinking claims already to *possess objectivity*. In a creed, in a life, in signs and wonders, somehow the divine has been definitively objectified in the world of fact. But critical thinking finds no sufficient reason to accept, and a strong case for rejecting, all such ideas. Yet it remains *objectively oriented in hope*. Where dogmatic thinking tries to stop the clock, critical thinking is historical. It moves forward by a continual relinquishing and receiving, letting go the old and awaiting the new.

In its continual exposure of religious anthropomorphism and illusion, its refusal to tolerate any other than a purely spiritual and transcendent God, its future orientation and demand for self-criticism, critical thinking has a notably prophetic quality. My claim is that a critical faith is possible, and that it is closer to biblical faith than is dogmatism.

Myth

Like religion, myth has been defined in a great number of ways because it is so pervasive and many-sided that it eludes capture in any single formula. Because western philosophy began precisely as a revolt against mythological ways of thinking, it still finds them hard to understand.

A myth is a story, and in particular a story of some religious importance. Myths may describe the birth of the gods, the establishment of the world order, the appearing of the first human beings, what happens to the dead, and how various social customs and institutions were established and why it is necessary to be loyal to them. Often myths seek to reconcile life's immemorial misdirection, paradoxes and conflicts, and may deal with the division of the sexes, the rivalry of tribes, moral evil and suffering, nature and society, and man and animal.

Now narrative is the literary form whose task is to explore the course and meaning of *human* life. Narrative deals with characters who live in time and subject to limitation, who are sentient rational agents interacting with each other, and so on. Narrative is essentially anthropomorphic, so that when gods, spirits, and monsters are made characters in a story they are inevitably represented as being something like humans. The use of myth in religion is therefore an attempt to impose a human likeness upon the inscrutable powers which govern human life, so that they can be at least partially understood and negotiated with on human terms. The social is projected or extended in the hope of encompassing and taming the supernatural. So, as a Jew would say, idolatry is the normal human condition, for man naturally tries to make the gods in his own image.

This helps to explain the connection between monotheism and history. Those who first believed in one God who was not human as we are, being Spirit and not flesh, needed a new kind of narrative to express their sense of the religious meaning of their lives. God could no longer appear as a character in the story visibly lending a hand, but had to be kept off the page as an almost-unmentioned observer of events. The tremendous narratives which describe the foundation and early history of the Israelite monarchy are so unmythological that they have been thought rather secular. God's government of events is kept veiled and largely unspoken—and history emerges.

But the urge to picture things divine in human terms is very strong and persists in some degree in all the great universal religions. In these faiths it was common to draw a contrast between this present fleeting world of the senses and a more perfect, divine and eternal world. Life's chief task was to gain salvation, conceived as a transfer from this world to the better world. And the persistence of mythological ways of thinking ensured that this better world was portrayed in terms drawn from the present one.

Of course the great faiths differ considerably in how large a part myth plays in them. Perhaps popular Hinduism is the most mythological, and the purest forms of Islam or early Buddhism the least. But every great tradition shows a history of conflict between mythical and anti-mythical strains. In Indian religion the attack on myth is carried out in order to eliminate distractions and purify spirituality. In the family of near-eastern monotheistic faiths the main emphasis is on purifying the concept of God. If God is infinite transcendent Spirit then God really is incomparable and can have no equal.

34

No story may be told in which God figures as a character alongside other characters, nor can any human language express what God is. One may even say that since God needs no environment it would be better to eliminate the meaning of heaven as the world God inhabits, and use the term simply as a reverential periphrasis for God.

So in ancient times people could only express what God is by the vehemence with which they repudiated every form of idolatry. In the age of classical theology the point was made by insisting on the primacy of the negative way (ultimately one can only say of God what God is *not*). And in the critical period we make the same point by insisting that religion is merely human and God is transcendent.

It is very difficult for theologians to be consistent here. Karl Barth, for example, clearly perceived the merely human character of religion, but still permitted himself to speak of God in mythological ways and always used the masculine pronoun to refer to God. I have eliminated it in this book.

Given the fact that monotheism must by its nature be continuously at war with mythological ways of speaking of God, it is very curious that Christianity should through most of its history have been as story-saturated as Hinduism. Most Christians remain unaware that they are regarded as idolaters by other monotheists, and though there have been some important iconoclastic movements in Christianity they have failed to strike really deep roots.

The main reason for this is naturally the enormous influence of the mythologized story of Christ and its effect upon the Christian understanding of God. Christians have come to think that the mythological habit of mind is correct in demanding a humanized deity. It is not clearly understood that in making such a demand one is turning away from monotheism and asking for a familiar human god instead of the one true God.

Jesus himself was stringently monotheistic and, as we shall see, his view of God was at the opposite pole from the weak anthropomorphism often attributed to him. But critical theology makes us aware that in the classic Christian creeds, liturgies, doctrinal definitions and theological treatises Jesus' own outlook and values have so far played little part. The myth has

35

largely obliterated the man. Critical faith, exposing the mythology, moves back towards monotheism and the real Jesus. Demythologizing is not clever sophistry, but a fundamental religious duty.

Eschatology

Theologians have a bad reputation for inventing jargon, but sometimes it is unavoidable. There is a highly important area of religious thought and experience which has been very largely lost in the modern west, and Christianity in particular cannot be properly understood without it. It is eschatology, from the Greek *ta eschata*, the last things. The traditional Four Last Things (death, judgement, heaven and hell) are associated with a late and individualized version of Christian eschatological teaching, but something rather closer to the biblical outlook survived until fairly recent times in such phrases as the Second Coming, the Advent hope, the millenium and the saints' everlasting rest, the Sabbath of the blessed.

The ultimate source of all these eschatological ideas is ancient and tribal man's experience of the cycle of the seasons. Each autumn the sun sinks lower in the sky, its vital energy declines, and the cosmic order slides towards decay and dissolution as the winter solstice approaches. But at the time of the solstice, or perhaps the vernal equinox, society enacts in a festival of faith and hope the death and passing of the old and the return and establishment of the new sun and new year.

Annually the cosmic order slips down to chaos and is restored, and historical man, with his much longer time-scale, begins to suspect that the occasional occurrence of great catastrophes such as earthquakes and floods points to a similar rhythm over a much longer period. World history on the largest scale may be cyclical, with gold, silver, bronze and iron ages succeeding each other until at last the whole cosmos is consumed by fire and reborn as the entire cycle begins again. This doctrine was probably originally consoling, for it explained suffering as part of a great cosmic process and promised that at the end of the long age of decline the cosmic conflagration would purify and renew the world, restoring it to its orginal perfection. But there were strong deterministic

36

overtones. Indian religious striving sought to escape from the great Wheel altogether, and Iranian thought appears to have held that there would be only one turning of the Wheel. After nine or twelve millenia the 'limited time' of history will be brought to an end, there will be a general Judgement, and the righteous will pass through to an 'unlimited time' of beatitude.

Ideas of the sort we have been discussing so far are to be found among the ancient Jews. The Psalter suggests that they may have kept an annual festival celebrating the enthronement of the Creator and the establishment of the cosmic order, and that ideas of the same kind also gathered around the coronation of a new king. But the Jews' distinctive achievement was to go still further than the Iranians in transferring their eschatological ideas from the realm of nature to that of history, and so to break free from cyclical thinking altogether. The one God does things once only, creating the world once, choosing one people, giving them one covenant, and directing their history towards one consummating moment of judgement and cosmic fulfilment. Jewish thought was resistant to ideas of reincarnation, whether in the present era, or by a cyclical return of the era, or in another universe. Its sense of the religious finality of this present life was so strong that it only slowly developed any ideas at all about the individual's destiny after death. The main emphasis was on the coming 'Day of the Lord' when God would rise up and act. Forces hostile to God would be overthrown, the creation would be brought to perfection and the faithful community would at last be finally vindicated by God. The bliss of this final consummation, the kingdom of God, was the supreme object of religious hope and the secret purpose of all history.

This very intense and specific form of eschatological hope is the fundamental presupposition of the rise of Christianity. There were various shades of emphasis, according to whether the kingdom was thought of in more worldly or otherworldly terms: it might be heralded by a great prophet, God might act through the person of a king like David, or there might be on standby in heaven a specially-empowered supernatural figure (who could be spoken of perhaps as the heavenly Messiah, the Son of Man or the Son of God) ready to be sent into the world to bring in the kingdom.

There could also be found a rabbinic idea of the kingdom of God which was more mystical than apocalyptic. The kingdom of God could be seen simply as God's rule within the heart of the devout individual believer. But on the evidence of the synoptic gospels, the Acts and Paul there can be little doubt that it was the eschatological idea of the kingdom rather than the rabbinic which dominated the outlook of the earliest Christians. They lived in the belief that the final consummation of the world was so close that it could be savoured and its powers were already manifest. Christianity cannot be understood unless one can imagine that first intense and burning joy.

The position of Jesus himself is a more difficult question, for many of the sayings attributed to him seem to presuppose the rabbinic rather than the eschatological picture of the kingdom of God. The precise mix of the rabbi and the prophet in Jesus himself vitally affects the interpretation of his teaching, and in particular the question as to whether Jesus himself can be a relevant teacher to us today.

During the present century many of the ablest scholars have broadly accepted two theses from the pioneers Johannes Weiss and Albert Schweitzer. The first thesis is that of 'consistent eschatology'; that the single idea underlying all Jesus' teaching is the coming of the kingdom of God, conceived in broadly apocalyptic terms. The second thesis is that this outlook cannot possibly be shared by modern man, and was indeed already fading and being transformed into something else in the lifetime of Paul. As late as 1950 Schweitzer was still putting the point starkly: 'From the second generation onwards the arrival of the kingdom becomes "one far-off divine event", and in later days it is infinitely far away . . . Originally it held a dominant position at the very centre of the faith; now it falls into the background.' (From an essay entitled 'The Conception of the Kingdom of God in the transformation of Eschatology', printed as an appendix to E. N. Mozley, *The Theology of Albert Schweitzer*, A. & C. Black 1950, page 82.)

If these theses are true without any qualification, then the original impetus of Christianity is irrecoverable, and what we now call 'Christianity' is a system of ideas considerably different from the faith of Jesus and his disciples. However, with regard to the first thesis there is a question about the precise

38

status of Jesus' teaching, and with regard to the second the abruptness and completeness of the loss of eschatology in Christianity should not be exaggerated. Millenarian movements have arisen constantly from the second century to the twentieth, and their characteristic doctrines could not be repudiated while they linger in the scriptures and creeds. Even within the mainstream, ardent eschatological hymns could still be written as late as the nineteenth century. Although Schweitzer was right to stress the importance of the theological change that began to take place towards the end of Paul's lifetime, we should not suppose that there was a single moment when Christianity permanently lost its original eschatological impetus. It has declined, it has been transposed, it has occasionally been revived, but it has hardly ever been quite forgotten. It could not be while the New Testament was still studied. I believe something important did happen around the year 1700, for at about that time people at last stopped believing that the world was hastening to an early end and a vista of indefinite progress through endless future time opened up. The subsequent rise of 'secular eschatologies' of progress and evolution posed severe problems for Christianity, but even then eschatological hope was not finally extinguished, and we should not assume that it cannot be recaptured.

Important though the Weiss-Schweitzer theses are, then, certain qualifications need to be made to them. Nineteenth-century thought was liberal, and liberalism becomes baffled and irritable in the face of a world-view which wholly rejects its own assumptions. The nineteenth century discovered the alienness of other cultures and world-views, but it was not very good at understanding them. Just as the first anthropologists said that tribal man's beliefs were factually mistaken, so the school of 'consistent eschatology' said that the outlook of Jesus and the first Christians was based on beliefs that were factually incorrect. In both cases it was too quickly assumed that the alien world-view could be dismissed.

The critical thinking which characterizes our own century is more receptive, more willing to have its horizons extended and less dogmatic about its own presuppositions. More pluralistic than the Victorians, we have learnt something of what it is to give up one whole way of looking at the world and open ourselves to a new. In the late liberal period, the last generation before 1914, the original message of Jesus seemed bizarre and incomprehensible. Today that is no longer so. The critical thinker, provided he really is willing to eliminate all elements of dogmatism from his own thinking, may find Jesus unexpectedly close, congenial and liberating.

And what of Jesus' mythology? It used to be said that Jesus was wholly committed to a mythological outlook which we cannot at all share. But there is a great difference between world-affirming mythology and world-ending mythology. Christendom made Christianity into a predominantly world-affirming mythology intended to validate the given cosmic, political and ecclesiastical order. The object was to fix and stabilize the world order and the social order. Jesus' world-ending mythology has exactly the opposite purpose, to free men from a world which is passing away and enable them to receive a coming new thing. I shall argue later that its inner meaning is not (in the pejorative sense) mythological at all.

So we must question a common assumption about the character of Jesus' message. The assumption is that it contained a prediction from which ethical commands followed, but the prediction turned out to be false and the commands are no longer relevant. Jesus predicted (so it is thought) a wholly transcendent divine event whose occurrence was in no way dependent upon human co-operation; but, given that that event was to take place, a certain human response was requisite. And since the event Jesus predicted has not taken place, all his teaching was based on a false assumption and so is not relevant to us.

This argument is still put forward, for example by Jack T. Sanders (*Ethics in the New Testament,* SCM Press, 1977). But it may rest upon a mistaken view of the logical character of prophecy. The language attributed to Jesus is intensely practical: he uses words to reveal, admonish, heal, promise, command, attack, pierce and console. It is not at all certain that forecasting is a prophet's central activity, for the case of Jonah reminds us that a prophet might succeed in his mission by being proved wrong in his forecast. Jonah's real mission was to *warn* successfully, not to *forecast* successfully.

The problem of the earliest Christian eschatology is not

easy, but for the moment I ask only that we should not give it up as insoluble. I shall propose a solution later.

Faith

The textbooks, which naturally enough reflect the dogmatic view of Christianity, distinguish two meanings of the word faith. The Faith, the objective content believed, is the whole body of supernaturally revealed truth contained in the Bible and the teaching of the church. Its counterpart in the self is faith the virtue, a humble trusting disposition of the soul by which one accepts God's revelation, obeys God's will and believes the Faith.

On this view of faith a final embodiment of divine truth is already established within the world of experience and defined in dogmatic propositions. The believer's part is to pray for the grace of acceptance and obedience. The free critical and sceptical spirit is ruled out as impious. Scholarship is tolerated only so long as it does not threaten orthodoxy: if it prudently confines itself to historical studies it is 'sound', but if it ventures into the area of doctrine and questions the received framework it is 'unsound'. The proper task of the Christian thinker is thought to be the defence of a citadel variously described as the Bible, the teaching of the church, or Holy Orthodox Tradition, against external critical assault. Among the defenders loyalty is regarded as the paramount virtue, and questions about whether it was wise to select this particular place for making the last stand are not appreciated. Great emphasis is placed on what is called 'objectivity', which in effect means taking it for granted that the citadel and the duty to defend it are absolutes.

However, citadel-dogmatism of this kind finds it notoriously difficult to avoid circularity and indeed emptiness. For the objectivity of the Faith requires that there be something which can be pointed to as the objective norm of faith, a rock against which the waves of critical questioning will beat in vain. Let us call this norm A. Then all our religious beliefs are verified by reference back to A, and in order to silence the critical questioner God must be invoked. What certifies A?—God does. How do we know what A means?—God will teach us, through the church. How can we come to believe *A*?—God will give us faith. And what is God?—*A* will tell us.

Here is another ring of arguments used in connection with the authority of the church in the seventeenth century, and of the Bible in the twentieth: We know from *A* that God is good. It is very bad for us to be without an objective norm of revealed truth, for it leads to all sorts of dissension and arbitrariness. So it is to be expected that God, being good, will have given us such a norm. Here is *A*, which claims to be the norm we need and expect to find. It is reasonable to accept *A* as our norm of religious truth—and *A* tells us that God is good, and does not leave us floundering in the darkness. For of course *A*'s testimony to itself is authoritative.

There is a paradox here, for dogmatic faith claims to be objective, definite and full of religious value, and yet as we study it it comes to seem oddly hollow. And conversely critical faith with its insistence that 'religion is human but God is transcendent' seems at first to be austere, negative and even empty, but on closer examination turns out to be the opposite.

The point is crucial and it is of course made repeatedly in the Bible. Faith in the living God is hard, so people tend to seek some kind of objective guarantee, relying on the Temple, or the monarchy, or their descent from Abraham, or ritual, or signs and wonders, or observance of the Law. But to speak of God as 'living' is to say that reliance on such guarantees is vain and ineffectual. 'Living' faith renounces them all. In Jesus' teaching religiosity in the form of orthodox belief and ultra-zealous observance is constantly seen as a barrier which men erect to defend themselves against the reality of God.

As Jesus shows, the mark of true faith is that it always demands a reversal of our natural expectations. And above all this reversal applies to the 'coming' of God of which he speaks. The natural tendency of the mind is to fancy that when God is far off God is strange, remote and mysterious, whereas when God comes near God becomes familiar, friendly and human. But the truth is the reverse. When God is kept at a distance behind a fence of ritual, rules and dogma, then God is humanoid and manageable. The remote God of mediated religion is comfortable and does not trouble us. But when ritual, rules and dogmas are overthrown and God comes near,

42

then the nearer God comes the more terrible, mysterious and alien God is. When God is most near, God is most purely transcendent.

Of course the Coming, the nearness and the farness here are mythological ideas, and what we are really speaking of is different forms of faith.

Dogmatic faith sets God behind a screen, and it imagines that the reality and objectivity of God are somehow given by the shape of the screen. The screen is regarded as sacrosanct, for it guarantees that God is real, gives an idea of what shape God is, and protects us against the reality of God. It is like the bandages and clothes wrapped around the Invisible Man in order to make him visible and so less threatening.

But God has no shape, and criticism exposes the merely human character of the screen. To overthrow it is an alarming exercise which people will certainly resist. But true prophetic monotheism is an attempt to live without the screen, and its modern equivalent is what I call critical faith.

Critical faith demands a certain ascetical rigour. It is all too easy for human beings to believe; what really requires courage is to learn to disbelieve. God is known by unknowing, believed in by disbelieving in all that is not God, and nearest when strangest. We raised an apparent paradox: if criticism is free and sceptical enquiry, and faith is humble, dogmatic and credulous, how can there be critical faith? And the resolution of the paradox is that critical faith is immediate, pure, spiritual and free precisely in its insistence on the transcendence of God, and its recognition of the merely human character of all our representations of God. The consummation of such a faith must be apocalyptic, for the natural grain of the self and the world are opposed to God, and the nearer God comes the more man and his world are confounded. Thus critical faith is not humanistic, like liberal faith, but ascetic: its highest object of hope is a perfect Coming of God which must overturn everything and wholly transform the self and the world. It cannot be fully realized in history for it is the end of history, but while we live in history it is a continually imminent challenge and ideal. It is the kingdom of God.

3

JESUS THE TEACHER

The Kingdom of God

In ancient Christianity the words of Jesus himself were invested with pre-eminent authority and ranked above the apostolic writings about him. Jesus was so much a man of the spoken word that a special respect for the oral tradition of his words continued (even though it was becoming increasingly garbled) long after the gospels were written. A memory of the former primacy of Jesus' words still survives today in the way the gospel ranks higher than the epistle in the Eucharistic liturgy.

This old tradition bears witness to the belief that the numinous, God-revealing and saving power of Jesus was most apparent in the way he used language. His words were charged with intense religious force which could transform the hearer. In those early days no one doubted that *sapientia* was more important than *scientia*, direct spiritual experience of the divine was more important than orthodox belief about divine things. But after the dogmatic definitions of the fourth and fifth centuries it began to look as if assent to the church's dogmatic beliefs about Jesus was more important and more necessary to salvation than being steeped in the words of Jesus, and so it remains to this day.

Several liberal theologians of the nineteenth century, following the lead given by F. D. E. Schleiermacher (1768–1834), did attempt to restore the teaching of Jesus to a central place in Christian theology. But the attempt backfired in a very curious way. The liberals saw that the central theme of Jesus' message had been the kingdom of God, and gave the concept a prominent place in their systems. Albrecht Ritschl, for example, saw the kingdom of God as the goal of history, an ideal

44

future moral community rather like Kant's kingdom of ends, which was gradually being realized by the action of human beings inspired by Christian love (*Justification and Reconciliation*, Eng. trans., 2nd edition, T. & T. Clark 1902, pages 8–14).

But this liberal and ethical interpretation of the kingdom of God was very sharply challenged when Ritschl's own son-in-law Johannes Weiss (whom we have already mentioned) published in 1892 *Jesus' Proclamation of the Kingdom of God*. Weiss thought that as a matter of historical honesty we ought to acknowledge that Jesus' notion of the kingdom of God had really been quite different from ours. For in Jesus' preaching it had been a thoroughly apocalyptic concept, a violent irruption of God into history to judge, destroy and transform the world-order. Weiss went very far, too far as it now seems, in emphasizing the wholly transcendent character of the kingdom. It was not anything to which human striving could contribute. No one, not even Jesus, could do more than watch and pray for its coming. Jesus had not taught an ethic of the kingdom but only an ascetical ethic for the time of waiting for it; his circle of followers were not the first citizens of the kingdom but merely lookouts; and Jesus himself was not yet Lord, Messiah or even Son of Man, but hoped to be given authority in the kingdom when it came. In the meanwhile his battle against Satan was not an active effort to establish the kingdom but merely a struggle to keep the enemy at bay during the period of waiting for God's final intervention.

However, Weiss still did not directly attack the modern liberal idea of the kingdom of God. As he himself put it:

This is not to say that one ought no longer to use the concept 'Kingdom of God' in the current manner. On the contrary, it seems to me, as a matter of fact, that it should be the proper watchword of modern theology. Only the admission must be demanded that we use it in a different sense from Jesus' . . . we do not share the eschatological attitude . . . another attitude has silently come among us in place of the strictly eschatological one . . . We do not await a Kingdom of God which is to come down from heaven to earth and abolish this world, but we do hope to be gathered with the Church of Jesus Christ into the heavenly (Kingdom). (*Jesus' Proclamation of the Kingdom of God,* Eng. trans. SCM Press 1971, pages 135f.)

In other words, critical honesty requires us to admit that modern Christianity is very remote from the outlook of Jesus himself, *and rightly so*. For Jesus' expectations were such as we cannot possibly share, and in any case he was mistaken. The liberal attempt to restore Jesus' message therefore collapsed when Weiss and later Schweitzer demonstrated just how remote from modern liberalism the real Jesus had in fact been. In the same year as that of Weiss' little book, Martin Kähler issued *The So-called Historical Jesus and the Truly Historic Biblical Christ* (Eng. trans. Fortress Press 1964) in which he argued that the chief topic of Christian preaching never was and never could be the Jesus of history, but the exalted Christ of church doctrine. So it seemed that on the one hand Jesus' own message was too remote and strange to be the basis of modern theology, and on the other hand that the starting-point of Christianity was in any case not so much Jesus himself as the theologized interpretation of him which arose in the early church.

All this set modern theology some very perplexing problems. Traditional Christian piety, deeply influenced by the gospel of John, had believed that the historical Jesus had actually and consciously been the incarnate Son of God who had come into the world to save men from sin and to found a church based on faith in himself as God's final saving revelation to men. In effect, Jesus had himself taught the classic Christian doctrines. But now this traditional piety had been falsified, not by external assault but by a careful reading of its own foundation documents. The Jesus of traditional Christianity and the Jesus of liberal Christianity had never existed. The real Jesus had been a charismatic prophet of the kingdom of God. He was a Jew, not a Christian, and his message was not Christian preaching. Christianity was still thought to be essentially a set of doctrines about Jesus, but it was now realized that they had been unknown to Jesus himself and arose only after his death. This set of doctrines, commonly styled the primitive Christian *kerygma* (or proclamation), is the true starting-point of Christianity and the basis upon which Paul, Augustine, Luther, Calvin and the moderns in turn built their systems of theology. As a corollary it follows that Christianity is under no special obligation to remain true to the outlook and values of Jesus himself, for the kerygma itself departs from his out-look. As Emil Brunner put it:

> It is of the very essence of revelation and of faith that we should become Christians not through the historical picture of Jesus, but through the picture traced by the gospels in the light of the Resurrection faith . . . The significance of Christ . . . is regarded by the church as a special revelation of God to the Apostles.

Brunner's point of view involves *denying* the ancient primacy of Jesus' own words. The epistles are rated higher than the synoptic gospels, and the apostolic church's doctrines about Jesus are seen as having more Christian substance in them than Jesus' own teaching. As Brunner adds, in a footnote on the same page:

> Hence, from the theological point of view the preference for the Synoptic Gospels evinced by theologians . . . is always a sign of bondage to the historical point of view. In faith we are not concerned with the Jesus of History, as historical science sees him, but with the Jesus Christ of personal testimony, who is the real Christ, and whom John shows us just as plainly—I could even say with Luther: still more clearly—as the Synoptists. (*The Mediator*, Eng. trans. Lutterworth Press 1934, page 159.)

How could Brunner, and many others with him, have said such a thing? It seeems that the essence of Christianity is still understood in doctrinal terms, and formal statements about God and God's action are rated as more important than the concrete experimental encounter with God in the words of the God-showing spiritual master.

The origins of Brunner's point of view go back to Lessing and Kierkegaard. Lessing remarked that Christianity requires us to believe some very strange doctrinal propositions and it offers historical evidence in support of those propositions. But historical evidence is never certain, only probable; so how could it ever be sufficient to justify an unconditional commit-ment to supernatural truths? (*Lessing's Theological Writings*, ed. H. Chadwick, A. and C. Black 1956, pages 51–56.) Kier-kegaard, in attempting to answer Lessing, was led to the furthest extreme of authoritarian fideism. In order to maintain faith's categorical demand, he stripped the content of Christ-ian faith of everything that could become a matter of learned

47

dispute and reduced it to one absolutely paradoxical proposition, that the God has become man; a proposition which confounds every human intellect equally in every generation. Before it the genius and the dolt, the Galilean disciple and the modern reader, are all exactly on a par. Kierkegaard does not altogether eliminate history, for he ties the absolute paradox to a particular man's life, but no amount of eyewitness observation of that life or critical study of the records of that life can do anything at all to explain or justify the impossible proposition which faith has to believe. 'Jurists say that a capital crime submerges all lesser crimes, and so it is with Faith. Its absurdity makes all petty difficulties vanish.' (*Philosophical Fragments*, Eng. trans. Princeton 1962, page 130; Kierkegaard is writing in the person of 'Johannes Climacus'.)

Twentieth-century theology has not gone quite as far as Kierkegaard, but it has learnt much from his solution. Historical criticism of Christian origins cannot make the venture of faith either more or less reasonable, for what faith believes is something supernaturally revealed. For Kierkegaard, what is believed is a single apparently self-contradictory proposition which cannot be made any less offensive by any amount of empirical information. For the moderns, what is believed is the kerygma of the church, which cannot be shown by historical investigation to be either a plausible or an implausible interpretation of Jesus of Nazareth, but must be accepted as revelation.

Disparagement of the historical (i.e. the real) Jesus and his message became for a time almost an orthodoxy. Jesus, it was said, was a Jew, not a Christian, and his preaching of the kingdom of God was part of Judaism, not of Christianity. The implications of this are markedly anti-Jewish: it is assumed that Christianity is absolutely discontinuous with Judaism, and if criticism establishes that Jesus belonged wholly to Judaism, then he must be expelled from Christianity in order to preserve intact the distinctively Christian (i.e. non-Jewish) way to salvation!

Rudolf Bultmann was pressed on this point. In his jargon the state of reconciliation with God which Christianity offers is called 'authentic existence'. So one may ask Bultmann in his own vocabulary, 'Did the preaching of Jesus make available to

48

the hearers of Jesus the possibility of authentic existence?', and Bultmann cannot and will not answer with a plain yes. In a Christian sermon it is not enough simply to present what Jesus said, for that would not be Christian preaching: it is necessary to present Jesus' message only in the context of the kerygma. But in denying that Jesus' words have saving power in their own right Bultmann was still subordinating religion to correct doctrine.

It seems that Jesus is only posthumously made into the pioneer of faith by the kerygma, so let us take the questioning a stage further. As a believing and practising Jew, Jesus had faith in God, prayed to God and so forth. Did Jesus himself therefore enjoy authentic existence? Was *he* saved by faith in the Christian manner? And again Bultmann will not say yes, for authentic existence by definition includes the conquest of the fear of death, and this conquest is possible only through the kerygma, which Jesus didn't know because it came into being only after his death, and in any case we do not know how Jesus saw his own death. So we cannot say confidently that Jesus enjoyed authentic existence; strictly speaking he is outside the gospel precisely because the gospel is a revelation, after his death, of the meaning of his death. (On all this see Norman Perrin, *Jesus and the Language of the Kingdom*, Fortress Press 1976, notes 55–56 on pages 185f.)

In the Middle Ages it was debated whether Jesus at the Last Supper offered a valid mass, but only in the present century has he been seen as outside Christianity. Theologians were driven to such an extreme by their desire to protect the nucleus of the dogmatic faith from historical criticism. Lessing had said two centuries ago, 'The religion of Christ and the Christian religion are two different things' (*op. cit.*, page 106), and theologians in the first half of this century decided to opt for the Christian religion and treat the religion of Jesus himself as pre-Christian.

This position, though adopted in response to critical questioning, was not itself critical, but dogmatic. It was dogmatism's last stand, and it was almost as fideistic and authoritarian as Kierkegaard has been, for it postulated a special revelation of Christianity to the post-Easter community, and there was no way of demonstrating by historical enquiry

49

the logic of the development from the message of Jesus to the kerygmatic message about him. If the continuity could be shown historically then it would undermine the pure givenness (i.e. groundlessness) of the revelation of the meaning of Jesus' life.

Dogmatism and a dualistic notion of truth thus entered with a vengeance. To the historian Jesus' life, message and death are events within the horizon of Judaism. But God subsequently announced that Jesus' life, message and death have a *different* meaning which transcends the bounds of Judaism. God's view of what Jesus means is quite discontinuous with the critical historian's view , and even quite discontinuous with Jesus' own view, and there is no way of showing that God's view is right and the critical view wrong or incomplete. God's revelation of the true significance of Jesus must simply be accepted as the beginning of Christianity. Modern theology felt the need for a very sharp dividing line between Judaism and Christianity, so it pushed the division forward from Jesus' nativity to Pentecost, moving Jesus himself back into Judaism and making the essence of Christianity a suprarational revelation of doctrines about him given to the post-Easter church.

Not surprisingly, since the critical spirit cannot simply give up, people did not remain content with this position for long. Critical Christian faith must resist attempts to preserve areas of faith exempt from criticism; it must be self-critical and seek to purge itself of all residual elements of dogmatism. Revelation is not a sheerly-given which defeats the critical spirit, but takes place in the ceaseless movement of the critical spirit itself. Now modern criticism has made it clear both that there is a real distinction between the Jesus of history and the Christ of faith, and that all theologies which start from the Christ of faith are dogmatic and not critical. Therefore critical faith must start from the Jesus of history as he and his message are made known to us by the critical historical method.

If Jesus, the real Jesus, is to be smuggled back into Christianity—not an easy thing to attempt—the coming of God's reign in Jesus' words must regain its proper precedence over the dogmas of the incarnation and the atonement and habitual assumptions about the relation of Christianity to Judaism. He and his message will not live for us until the stiff ancient
50

cerements wrapped about him by the centuries are stripped away.

The neo-orthodox reply, as the orthodox always have done, that the summons to faith is urgent and cannot wait for the scholars to complete their critical enquiries. Those enquiries will go on for ever and still only yield an approximation. So Kierkegaard says that 'this wishful hypothesis, this beautiful dream of critical theology, is an impossibility . . . because an approximation is the only certainty attainable for historical knowledge—but also an inadequate basis for an eternal happiness' (*Concluding Unscientific Postscript*, Eng. trans. Princeton University Press 1941, page 31). Like so many philosophers of the past, Kierkegaard summons up the spectre of scepticism and the endless regress in order to frighten his readers into dogmatism. In order to realize the relation to God, he thought, human thinking must 'transcend itself in the paradoxical. And Christianity is precisely the paradoxical,'—i.e. dogmatism (*ibid.*, page 95). But on the contrary, I suggest that human thinking transcends itself in the critical, that is, when it has become fully conscious of itself, has purged itself of all residual elements of dogmatism, and fully accepts that it is indeed only an approximation. Only then is it naked and free before the true God who is Spirit, and ready to hear God's word in Jesus' words.

Lessing said—adapting, perhaps, a saying of Meister Eckhart (Fragment 18 in Eng. trans. by R. B. Blakney *Meister Eckhart: A Modern Translation,* Harper Torchbook edn. 1957, page 240)—that if God held all truth in his right hand, and in his left hand held the lifelong pursuit of it, he would choose the left hand. This is playing odds and evens with God, objects Kierkegaard (*ibid.* page 97), and so it would be if we were offered the choice, but we are not. God holds out to us only the left hand: that is why there is not and cannot be a last book of theology or of philosophy, in spite of all the attempts to write them. Even Kierkegaard's protest against critical theology, that it can only yield an approximation, rebounds upon itself and is itself made into a mere approximation by the passage of time. In this life we are *in via*, on the way, so that a continuously shifting approximation is indeed appropriate to our condition. And precisely in the consciousness that we are but

51

approximating lies our indirect knowledge of that to which we approximate. All refusal to accept approximation is dogmatism and cannot stand.

If critical theology is to return to Jesus himself it must of course accept the results of critical study of the gospels. We have only the barest outline of his life and nothing or next to nothing of his personality, but we do have a substantial tradition of his teaching and of the kinds of activity he engaged in. Limited though our knowledge is, the main themes of his life and message have survived. They are three in number:

First, Jesus was a charismatic prophet of the kingdom of God. He did not act as God's mouthpiece and deliver oracles prefixed by the formula, 'Thus says the Lord,' in the manner of the classic prophets of old, but he and his sometime master John the Baptist were both prophets according to the criteria current in their day. Jesus and the Baptist stongly recall the Elijah and Elishah sagas. Jesus' commissioning as a prophet is linked by the gospels with his baptism, at which a heavenly voice (*bath kol*) attests his mission and he is filled with the divine Spirit. His task as a prophet was to announce, to prepare men for and (in a sense to be defined) to be the midwife of, to reveal or inaugurate, the reign of God.

Secondly, in close connection with his prophetic mission, Jesus was also an exorcist and healer.

Finally, the title Rabbi (*Mar, Kyrios*, etc., i.e. Master, Lord, Teacher) was applied to him. There was not yet an institutional rabbinate, so the meaning is that Jesus was a spiritual master and a teacher of Wisdom. (The classic Jewish Wisdom writings include Job, Proverbs, Ecclesiastes, Ecclesiasticus and the Wisdom of Solomon. Their main concern is with morality and piety. The memory of Jesus as a teacher of Wisdom was preserved in Paul's description of him as 'the Wisdom of God' in 1 Corinthians.)

Even this minimal statement of the three main themes of Jesus' life already raises a difficulty. To a wise man or spiritual master the relation of the self to God is timeless, and he is not usually historically or dispensationally minded. So for rabbinic and talmudic Judaism the kingdom of heaven is simply faith in God, the rule of God over the human heart. Merely to say the *Shema* twice daily ('The Lord our God, the Lord is

52

One') is to take upon oneself the yoke of the kingdom of heaven, that is, to let God reign in one's heart (e.g. C. G. Montefiore and H. Loewe, *A Rabbinic Anthology*, Macmillan 1938, page 3.) But the eschatological prophet by contrast is intensely historically and dispensationally minded. For him the kingdom of God is a coming new world-order. So how can Jesus have joined elements of *both* outlooks? They seem incompatible.

It is, I suppose, conceivable that Jesus' message was internally incoherent. But it is unlikely, and in general it is a sound critical principle that an interpreter should prefer a coherent interpretation as being more probable than an incoherent one. In the case of Jesus there is one valuable clue; the all-important theme of reversal runs through both his eschatological teaching and his ethical Wisdom teaching and is the key, as we shall see, to his message as a whole.

It is necessary—though, to a non-specialist like myself, daunting—to say roughly what material one provisionally accepts as authentic. Following and slightly adapting Norman Perrin (*op. cit.*), one might list it as follows, under four heads:

(a) *Kingdom Sayings*

1. 'But if it is by the finger of God that I cast out demons, then the kingdom of God has come upon you.' Luke 11:20.
2. 'The kingdom of God is not coming with signs to be observed; nor will they say, "Lo here it is!" or "There!" for behold, the kingdom of God is in your midst.' Luke 17:20–21.
3. 'Why does this generation seek a sign? Truly, I say to you, no sign shall be given to this generation.' Mark 8:12.
4. 'From the days of John the Baptist until now, the kingdom of heaven has suffered violence, and men of violence plunder it.' Matthew 11:12.

The general drift of these sayings is fairly clear. Jesus is not specifying and carrying out a schedule of apocalyptic events, but saying that the *summum bonum*, the kingdom of God, is already present to those who have eyes to see. Battle between two opposite orders of things is already joined, and the afflictions of the Baptist and of Jesus and his circle, and the exorcisms performed by Jesus, are episodes in that great conflict.

The range of Jesus' thought extends from apocalyptic to

53

Wisdom, and what links these two extremes is his experience of the last battle between good and evil and of the reign of God as already present though hidden realities. The conflict between the two world-orders (apocalyptic) is already going on within the human heart (wisdom), or to put it the other way round, in Jesus' ministry the perennial confrontation of man with God (wisdom) is intensified to its final (apocalyptic) level.

(b) *The Lord's Prayer* Luke 11:2–4.

In successive clauses the prayer expresses the devout man's intimate fellowship with God, the divine transcendence, a longing to see God's reign, faith's utter dependence upon God, the identity of religious and moral categories, and a cry for preservation in the final conflict.

(c) *The Proverbial Sayings* (Bultmann's selection: see his *The History of the Synoptic Tradition*, Eng. trans. Basil Blackwell 1963, esp. page 105.)

1. DEMAND 'Leave the dead to bury their dead.' Luke 9:60. 'If anyone strikes you on the right cheek, turn to him the other also,' etc. Matthew 5:39b–41.

2. REVERSAL 'For whoever would save his life will lose it; and whoever loses his life (for the sake of the kingdom of God) will save it.' Mark 8:35 (reconstructed).

'How hard it will be for those who have riches to enter the kingdom of God . . . It is easier for a camel (rope?) to go through the eye of a needle,' etc. Mark 10:23b, 25.

'Many that are first will be last and the last first.' Mark 10:31.

'Everyone who exalts himself will be humbled, and he who humbles himself will be exalted.' Luke 14:11.

3. CONFLICT 'No one can enter a strong man's house and plunder his goods, unless he first binds the strong man,' etc. Mark 3:27.

'If a kingdom is divided against itself,' etc. Mark 3:24–26.

4. EXHORTATIONS 'No one who puts his hand to the plough and looks back is fit for the kingdom of God.' Luke 9:62. 'Enter by the narrow gate,' etc. Matthew 7:13–14.

'There is nothing outside a man which by going into him can defile him; but the things which come out of a man are what defile him.' Mark 7:15.

'Whoever does not receive the kingdom of God like a child shall not enter it.' Mark 10:15.

'Love your enemies,' etc. 'You therefore must be perfect, as your heavenly Father is perfect.' Matthew 5:44–48.

(d) *The Parables*

J. D. Crossan, as cited by Perrin, classifies them as follows:

1. PARABLES OF THE COMING OF THE NEW WORLD The fig tree, the leaven, the sower, the mustard seed, the lost sheep, the coin.

2. PARABLES OF REVERSAL The good samaritan, the rich man and Lazarus, the Pharisee and the publican, the wedding guests, the proper guests (Luke 14:12–14), the great supper, the prodigal son.

3. PARABLES OF ACTION The wicked husbandmen; and eight servant-parables: the doorkeeper (Mark 13:34), the overseer (Luke 12:42–46), the talents, the throne claimant (Luke 19:12b, 14–15a, 27), the unmerciful servant, the servant's reward (Luke 17:7–10), the unjust steward, the workers in the vineyard.

Naturally, this list of the most probably authentic elements in the tradition is open to dispute at many points. Some of the 'redaction critics' hold that Matthew and Luke cannot supply us with *any* authentic material beyond what they reproduce from Mark. If they are right then the list would have to be reduced severely, being confined to what can be recovered from a critical study of Mark. But even in that case, with a very reduced body of material, the gist of the message would remain substantially the same.

In any attempt to express the message it must be recognized that its most essential feature is the linguistic form in which it is cast. Jesus nowhere speaks the language of systematic theology, nor does he describe the polity of the kingdom. His teaching is not dogmatic. The discontinuity between the old world which is passing away and the new world into which he is attempting to induct his hearer is so great that language will not, so to speak, carry through from the former to the latter. Hence he must use language in odd ways, invoking a very large number of strange rhetorical devices which are still not fully analysed by scholars. The telling of a parable was not just the setting up of a revelatory religious image, but rather a

55

linguistic action intended to produce an imaginative shock and so facilitate in the responsive hearer the change needed if he was to receive or enter the kingdom.

Some critics who are very conscious of the limits of historical knowledge and the problem of historical relativity urge, first that we do not know and cannot know exactly what Jesus meant by the kingdom of God, and secondly that even if we did know exactly what he meant by it that meaning would inevitably belong to his time and cultural setting and not ours. But this criticism can be met by pointing out that the expression 'the kingdom of God' does not in the ordinary sense *have* a meaning. It does not signify a state of affairs which can be described in language. It is *that which a certain set of linguistic techniques shows to and actualizes in a receptive hearer*. It is not a culture-bound concept but that which transcends any and every historical 'cultural totality', for it is after all the end of the world.

If—perish the thought!—Jesus were to be thought of as a theologian, it would have to be as a theologian of the negative way. What is objectively the kingdom of God is subjectively simply the relation to God. And for him the true relation of the self to God cannot be attained by any affirmation of images, by any confirmation or extension of the existing social and religious order, or by any extrapolation of our ordinary ways of thinking. On the contrary, his images are of cosmic war, destruction and transformation; of complete abandonment of the whole traditionally hallowed ritual and social order, and of eschatological reversal. We do not enter upon the relation to God until we have radically relativized, abandoned and come to regard as fleeting and foolish our whole world; 'world' here meaning both our standard and received conceptual framework and the picture of reality which it generates. God is transcendent and God's arrival annihilates all else. Then only the relation to God matters; its demand overrides all else and simply wipes out all relativities. Ruthless and drastic action becomes imperative.

We began with two views of the kingdom, that of Ritschl who saw it as created by human moral effort, and that of Weiss who saw it as a future and catastrophic world-ending event brought about by God to which human effort could contri-

56

bute nothing. But we can now see that it is wrong to imagine that where God does everything man does nothing and vice versa. The perfect world is pure gift and it costs everything; the realization of the kingdom of God is God's absolute action and man's too, for it demands of man that absolute and unique act which transcends or negates all other forms of action, the act of faith.

Critical Christian faith understands the relation to God, and the sovereignty of God, in the way taught and exemplified by Jesus of Nazareth. Jesus did not teach doctrines about the kingdom, but used language in such a way as to actualize it in the receptive hearer. It is above all in his words that he is the kingdom-bringer or Messiah.

How God Is Shown

In Christianity the centrality of Jesus as revealer of God is expressed by a variety of idioms—God is the Father of Jesus, Jesus is the only Son of God, prayer is made to God through Jesus Christ—all of which suggest that for Christians Jesus determines the way God is to be understood and approached. So it is very surprising that the ways Jesus showed God in his teaching have so far exercised little influence upon Christian thought. It is difficult to think of any Christian account of God which has been at all closely or strictly modelled upon Jesus' teaching style. Perhaps Christian existentialism has come nearest to attempting it, but more often mythology prevails and the fact that Jesus shows God's nearness is taken as making it legitimate to think of God as somehow human and like Jesus—which is very far from Jesus' actual teaching.

Now a critical approach to Christianity must be based on the historical Jesus, in spite of the fact that this leads one into 'heresy' because from early times Christianity began to drift away from the real Jesus. There is no other possible starting-point than the real Jesus, because the alternatives always involve fideism and authoritarianism.

However, it is immediately objected that we do not know enough about Jesus to be able to base a defensible account of Christianity upon him. How decisive is this objection? It is

57

perfectly true that our historical knowledge of Jesus is very limited, for only the barest outlines of his life and personality survive, but the legacy of the real Jesus is not so much his person as his teaching, and of that we have a substantial tradition, preserved almost entirely in the synoptic gospels of Matthew, Mark and Luke. Just how much of this material can be confidently ascribed to Jesus himself we shall never know with certainty. But this does not matter quite as much as might be thought. Suppose that the whole body of material comprising individual sayings parables and so forth contains about 1,000 items; and suppose that a very conservative critic regards some 700 items as original and a radical critic regards only some 70 items as original. Still, the long list and the short list will in practice be found to resemble each other sufficiently for the two critics to be in a large measure of agreement about the main lines of Jesus' message.[1] Even the most radical critic does not doubt that the real Jesus was much more like the Jesus of Mark than the Jesus of John, that he spoke in parables, that the principal theme of his message was the kingdom of God, and so on.

Furthermore, we have suggested that Jesus' teaching about God is given not in dogmatic instruction, but rather in the distinctive linguistic techniques he employed to induct people into or to reveal the reign of God. It is clear from the synoptic gospels that there is in the tradition of his teaching a set of such techniques, and that understanding of them was preserved for some time after his death. The linguistic techniques imply a religious outlook, and they are much more certain than particular sayings. Thus, that Jesus spoke in parables is much more certain than it is that he spoke any particular parable. A critical Christian theology will pay close attention to these techniques, and consider what is implied in the choice of them. The only odd feature of such a programme is that it has so rarely been attempted.

To regard the teaching of Jesus as fundamental to Christian faith is not to view Jesus himself dogmatically. To be true in philosophy to the spirit of Socrates is not to regard Socrates dogmatically, for Socrates himself stands precisely for the

[1] Compare, for example, the accounts of Jesus' message given in the New Testament theologies of R. Bultmann and J. Jeremias.

anti-dogmatic principle. Similarly, Jesus himself is critical in that for him God is beyond the reach of ordinary language and worldly ways of thinking, and can only be elicited or shown by odd rhetorical devices. He too says that 'religion is human but God is transcendent'. And he himself demands a free imaginative response from his hearer. His way to God and revelation of God can be and must be continually rediscovered experimentally, and it may well be that there are some aspects of his thought and outlook (though not the most fundamental) in which the critical mind cannot now join him, such as his apparent belief in demons. So critical obedience to him is not and cannot be slavish, or it would not be obedience to *him*.

What then does Jesus' teaching imply about God? Much that he has to say is clearly in the great tradition of prophetic Judaism. God is Creator; God's claims override all others; the relation to God demands not just external observance but a radical turning of the whole self, mind and heart, to God; and in this turning—which Jesus intensifies to the point where it becomes the great eschatological reversal, a cosmic turning upside-down—salvation, grace and forgiveness are received. The devout believer learns that he gains by losing, lives by dying. In wholly submitting to God's judgement he receives God's salvation.

In this way Jesus did more than continue the tradition of the prophets: he finalized it. His intense eschatological awareness led him to press the prophetic message to the point at which it broke through into a gospel of salvation. Jesus preached the full and final gospel of eschatological salvation by faith. Many exegetes have, I think, been restrained by their inherited Protestant faith from recognizing this, for they have thought that the full gospel of salvation by faith presupposes the death and resurrection of Jesus. But in fact Jesus preached the death and resurrection of the self as the true and final way to God before following it himself. It was only because he first proclaimed the way and then followed it that the early church was able to recognize him as being himself the Way.

More of this later. Meanwhile, what was there that was most distinctive in Jesus' view of God? The impression is prevalent that he encouraged an extreme, not to say infantile anthropomorphism—childlike, simple faith in God as Father.

59

Now there can be little doubt that the historical Jesus did indeed speak of God às Father (Abba), and that for him as for the Hasidim[1] generally, the immediate inner communion of the individual with God was supremely important. But merely to say this is to miss his real message. Joachim Jeremias has strongly emphasized Jesus' sense of a filial relation to God, but in his analysis of 'Ways of Speaking preferred by Jesus' he puts at the head of the list *the divine passive*. By this he means that, as with some other Jewish teachers, Jesus' sense of the divine holiness and transcendence is so great that he prefers not to speak of divine action in any open or direct way, but to use various circumlocutions. The way God works is so different from any human working that one does not speak of it univocally or even analogously, but in a veiled, indirect and negative way. So in the second half of a beatitude God's name is not expressly mentioned: 'Blessed are they that mourn, for they shall be comforted', but how and by whom may not be openly said.

Jeremias lists no less than eighteen different forms of circumlocution for God in the synoptic tradition, and about a hundred uses of the single most important form, the divine passive (*New Testament Theology*, volume 1, Eng. trans. SCM Press 1971, pages 8ff.). The nearest parallel to such an extensive use of the idiom is in apocalyptic literature, which similarly stresses the divine transcendence and the unlikeness between ordinary worldly action and God's action.

Two other certainly authentic features of Jesus' utterance are highly relevant here. The first is his use of *antithetic parallelism*: sayings typically in two branches, of which the second is a kind of reversal of the first, and very often the accent or punch of the saying is in the second branch. Examples are to be found in the reversal sayings quoted earlier. Jeremias lists 118 such sayings in the tradition, and points out that (like the divine passive) they are about equally distributed among the four main strata of the tradition: Mark; Matthew and Luke; Matthew only; and Luke only. Jeremias notes that this linguistic form occurs both in wisdom and in apocalyptic literature,

[1]The *Hasid*, the poor saint, is the ideal type of Jewish believer, and the inspiration of many movements in Judaism. Compare New Testament ideas of the poor and the saints.

and in general no scholar can doubt that Jesus made exception-
ally extensive use of it. The theological point is that this
linguistic form again expresses Jesus' sense of discontinuity:
divine things are no sort of prolongation of human things (as
in the 'synonymous parallelism' of much devotional literature), but a startling reversal of them. It is at this point that we
can glimpse something of the unity of Jesus' message, and how
the wisdom element of ethical teaching and spiritual direction
coheres with the eschatological element. If a man is to know
God, or to enter the reign of God, there has to be a violent
disruption or reversal of his world-outlook. It is called
metanoia or repentance, and is so great an event that it may be
spoken of objectively as the end of the world, or subjectively
as the loss of one's life and the death of the self, so that the new
world and the new self may be born. In terms of Wisdom,
Jesus' message seeks to change the self. But he did not just give
private instruction to selected pupils; he addressed the nation,
and that public prophetic mission was a call to a new world.
His teaching can be and should be read at both levels.

The prominence of antithetic parallelism in Jesus' message
is in marked contrast to later attempts to create a Christian
humanism which moves on the basis of analogy from the
natural order to the order of grace without a catastrophic
break. It is true that occasionally Jesus is shown as using
synonymous parallelism, but he barbs it. For example, the
'how much more' sayings (Matthew 6:30 = Luke 12:28;
Matthew 7:11 = Luke 11:13) are set in contexts where Jesus
draws analogies from nature and human nature to commend
faith in God's providence, but even here he does not fail to
stress human wickedness and faithlessness and how difficult it
is to believe anything so simple without a complete change of
heart.

Secondly, there is Jesus' distinctive use of *parables of the
kingdom*: parables expressing the nearness of the kingdom—so
close, so secret, so great—its apparently outrageous demand
and the shock it gives to our ordinary assumptions and expectations. The themes of reversal and discontinuity appear again
here, and the oft-repeated observation that the parables are not
allegories or analogies makes the point that God is not to be
read off them as a quasi-human character in an allegorical

61

story. The parables do not communicate descriptive information about God, but rather seek to provoke a response to God's sudden, irrupting presence.

But there is a more subtle point, less easy to notice, and this point I have to make by producing an analogy.

Great comedy—for example, in Mozart's operas—is a very serious business. It will not tolerate the slightest lapse of taste. Flawless, utterly sure-footed evenness of tone and style must be maintained. The characters must enact their timelessly absurd roles of ardent lover, jealous father-figure, reluctant maiden, wily servant and so on with a finely tuned appearance of conviction. The characters must not overtly laugh either at each other or at themselves, for that would spoil the joke. The humour is distilled to its most transcendent and painful purity by never appearing. The plot must develop with rigorous yet preposterous inevitability. The flow of bubbling high spirits is kept pure and steady by the unquestioning seriousness with which all the characters take their absurd roles and the iron-butterfly logic of the conventions.

As the joke must be hidden in comedy, so God must be hidden in the parables. The characters in comedy must not profess to see the joke: the joke is best revealed by being kept hidden, suspended invisibly in dramatic irony. The entranced spectator knows he shares the joke with the actors, but the joke is only maintained so long as there is no nudging. The game must not be given away. And of course in comedy there is a good deal of reversal—reversal of sex roles, reversal jokes (as for example in Wilde), and reversal, in the conventions, of the way we know things to be in real life.

This analogy sheds some light of Jesus' message. The Jewish tradition has long been permeated by humour. As the first monotheists, the Jews had always recognized the terrifying holiness, greatness and utter incomprehensibility of God, but they also had in their tradition a belief in the possibility of direct, unmediated fellowship between man and God. The co-existence of these two themes could give rise to a demand for a mediator to make the encounter of man with God less painful, as smoked glass makes it easier for the eye to gaze at the sun. But if one could avoid that temptation the alternative was humour, the highest spiritual achievement of Jewish religion. Because God and man are such preposterously unequal partners, their relationship must be comical. Man's idea of God must fall absurdly short of the reality of God, and his religious behaviour cannot but be objectively absurd.

In Jesus this traditional Jewish sense of the incongruity between man and God was bound to reach a climax. The tradition of his teaching shows that he had an exalted and almost apocalyptic awareness of the transcendence of God, and that he believed in the possibility of intimate communion with this God. Thus much of his teaching has a *stringently humorous character*. He does not speak about God directly but rather shows God by the way he represents, and invites his hearer to perceive, man's absurdity in the face of God. For it is only by a humorous perception of himself that a man can repent and enter upon a right relation to God. The kind of insight needed to see that God is upon me is rather like the kind of insight needed to see that the joke is upon me.

So Jesus described the absurdity of man before God. When the message of the arrival of God is preached people will do almost anything to resist responding to it. When told of the nearness and greatness of God they say, 'Thank you, that was very interesting. Now if you will excuse me, I have a few things to attend to, I've just married, there's a funeral, I've bought a pair of oxen and must try them out.' They are perfectly decent orthodox believers, but they would prefer God to stay some distance off and let them get on with their own lives. They are the healthy, those who are so busy with little things that they have no time for important things. They are sincerely apologetic about this state of affairs, and cannot imagine how it has come about, but they never quite seem able to find the time to do anything about it. So long as God obligingly remains distant they continue to pass for healthy, but as God comes nearer they look more and more absurd. By contrast the sick and the troubled seem morbid at ordinary times, but the closer God comes the more sensible they look. The arrival of God thus reverses ordinary human valuations; sensible, self-absorbed and busy people begin to look ridiculous, and sick and needy people begin to look sensible.

It is well known that Jesus took this principle of the reversal of values to extraordinary lengths, and applied it not just to the world of men without God but to the world of religion as well. Harlots go into the kingdom of God ahead of the devout. A devout man who can truly say to God that he is pious and righteous is lost, whereas a poor wretch who knows that he is lost is saved. Here is the solution of the paradox of Jesus' attitude to the Pharisees. Of course they were the best of the parties in contemporary Judaism and the people closest to Jesus himself, and for that very reason he satirizes them, for the arrival of God confounds not just the worldly and not just false religion, but even true religion. An antinomian streak appears in Jesus' attack on all calculation of moral differences between men. In the face of the arrival of God any attempt to deflect God by comparing ourselves with other people instead of with God is exposed as an absurd evasion. Jesus' satirical attack on human moral calculation is particularly vivid in the recommendations about where to sit at a dinner party and how to see clearly to remove a speck from your neighbour's eye, and in the parable of the dishonest steward.

All this must make one question the very idea of a Christian morality which establishes a comfortable continuity between the realms of nature and grace, and sets up a nicely graduated scale of religious duties. But there is worse to come in Jesus' mockery of men's ideas about God. When he recommends people to think of God as an unjust judge, as a father who prefers the scapegrace to the loyal son and as an employer who pays workers without regard to the hours they have worked, he confounds any attempts to move by the rules of analogy from human justice to divine. God sends the rain on the just and the unjust alike, and prefers the lost to the safe, the sick to the healthy, and sinners to the righteous. Religious observances are so perilous to the soul that all of them, prayer, fasting and almsgiving, must be performed secretly and even unconsciously, so that your right hand does not know what your left hand is doing.

Critical honesty obliges me to remark before I become carried away that this truly remarkable line of irony is most highly developed in specifically Lucan material, and so may be attributable not to Jesus himself but rather to the redactor of Luke's gospel. However, there is enough of it in the other strata of the tradition for one to be reasonably confident that

64

the main themes I have just laid out do go back to Jesus himself. And in any case the author of Luke may simply have been more highly sensitive than the other evangelists to a key element in the tradition he received.

So then, four of the best attested and most important features of Jesus' utterance, his use of the divine passive, of antithetic parallelism, of parables, and of humour, convey in an indirect way a good deal of teaching about God and man's relation to God. We have in the tradition as a whole about 100 examples of the first, 120 of the second and 40 or more of the third. The style of humour that I have described cannot be quantified but is pervasive. It is within this massive body of material that Jesus' message about God is implicit, and since the material is broadly consistent and evenly distributed through all the strata of tradition, critical purging of it is unlikely to alter very much the shape of what it communicates. And it is the background against which Jesus' use of the term 'Father' for God has to be understood. Without that background it becomes infantile pietism, but properly understood against that background it becomes something entirely different. It is sometimes fancied that the God of the Old Testament is remote and dreadful, and the God of the New near and familiar. That is wrong. Jesus' emphasis on the holiness and transcendence of God, the disjunction of things divine and things human, the mysteriousness of divine action and the confounding unexpectedness of divine grace is no weaker than but fully as strong as anything in the tradition from which he sprang. His God is as dreadful as the God of Moses, and yet the devout disciple who longs for God's reign can, in secret only, commune with and address this God as Father.

In Christianity it is said that Jesus Christ is God's only Son. This expression should not be understood, as it too often is, in a pagan or Gentile manner. What it means is that the God of Christians is defined as the one whom Jesus believed in and disclosed in his teaching. He is the one mediator, whose faith in God and ways of showing God are taken to be definitive and exemplary. But his mediation should not be understood in any way that diminishes the lethal, salutary shock of the self's encounter with God.

Socrates is more like Jesus than is Plato, and Kierkegaard is more like Jesus than is Hegel, for Jesus is a critical or dialectical teacher, and not a dogmatic instructor. Jesus does not teach a doctrine of God, for what God is cannot be communicated directly but only shown indirectly by the teacher's choice of strategies. What Jesus had to say could only be said in the ways he chose for saying it. The God of Jesus is pure Spirit, hidden, sovereign, free, and knowable only by the peculiar mental switch I once called 'the leap of reason' and which the Greek New Testament calls *metanoia*, or repentance. The hiddenness of God Jesus expresses in his use of the divine passive, the switch by his use of antithetic parallelism, the contrast between the old world and the new age by his use of parables, and the collision between the self and God by his use of humour.

There is an intimate connection between Jesus' use of apocalyptic and eschatological ideas and his discovery of salvation by faith. He cannot be called strictly an apocalyptic thinker, for he was not interested (according to the evidence we have) in pseudonymous writing, or in scheduling the Last Things, or in fantastic visions of world history, or in esoteric symbolism; but he surely does share something of the apocalyptists' dualism ('God has made not one world but two' —2 Esdras 7:50) and of their understanding of God. The God of apocalyptic is hidden, transcendent and sovereign, and brings in the new world without human aid. When the old world comes to an end everything that can give me any confidence to stand before God is wiped out. My work, my achievement is gone and I am left naked and dependent only on God's inscrutable mercy. If I am saved it will be God's work entirely and in no sense at all my own accomplishment. Thus the idea of salvation by faith is reached by *internalizing and intensifying apocalyptic,* discarding its frivolous visions of world history, its bizarre symbolism, and its revelations of secret knowledge, and keeping only what is of real religious value, the confrontation of the naked individual with the immediate presence of God Almighty: 'the reign of God is at hand.' Jesus' aim is to drive home the magnitude of the crisis, and the idioms he uses show that the God who is near is not the cosy God of family piety but the terrible God who reduces the world to ashes and the self to dust.

And so to return at last to our starting point, we now have a context in which to answer the question, did Jesus teach the fatherhood of God? And the answer is yes; but God is known as Father only by those in whom all earthly conceptions of fatherhood, authority and the like have been burnt out by the confrontation with God. Unlike Elijah's disciple Elishah (1 King 19:19–21), James and John do not even say farewell to their father Zebedee (Mark 1:19–20). There is not time. And Jesus is constantly reported as stressing the discontinuity between human fatherhood or authority and divine, often in extremely harsh terms (e.g. Matthew 10:34–37, 19:29, 23:9; Luke 14:26, etc.). In the narratives of Jesus' adult life his father is absent and his mother quickly repudiated (Mark 3:31–35). Not all of this is historical, but much of it has the authentic ring: the arrival of the reign of God overrides even the most sacred obligations of the old world-order.

It is certainly true, then, that the devout individual's secret communion with God was important to Jesus; but it is also true that the tradition of his teaching emphasizes the transcendent holiness of that God, and the greatness of God's demand upon the individual. Traditional Christianity interposed the risen Christ between man and God. Christ was used as a lightning-conductor, to take away the shock of the soul's encounter with God. Christ was to be a friendly, human god. But the real Jesus had not the slightest intention of diminishing in any way the shock of the encounter with God. On the contrary, he emphasized it to the highest degree. Nothing could be more false to him than to make of him the principal object of worship, and use him as a shield against the reality with which above all else he sought to confront men.

The Message and the Messenger

It is often argued that the critical attempt to recover the message of Jesus leads to a dead end. We use the critical method to recover what he was saying, and discover a message which though it may be admired aesthetically cannot be appropriated, for it incorporates as an essential element a precritical understanding of myth.

I have replied that the key to the message is the linguistic

67

form in which it is cast. Jesus reaches into a world in which people are comfortably getting on with their lives without God, and borrows its imagery only to blow it up. His way to God is implicit in his techniques for exploding his hearer's godlessness. Indeed, words like 'message' and 'teaching' can be misleading, for Jesus is hardly at all concerned with giving information or making predictions. On the contrary, his speech is religious action: he warns, summons, reveals, commands, promises and attacks, always with the intention of bringing about religious change in the hearer. It is a mistake to see him as culture bound, for his words were aimed at releasing the hearer from every form of cultural bondage or worldliness: the call was to abandon *everything* and receive the reign of God.

So it is somewhat beside the point to suggest that his message turns on factually incorrect beliefs about future events. He declined to offer signs and professed ignorance about timings, or so at least Mark says (8:12, 13:32). His style was eschatological rather than apocalyptic. For him the relation to God can only begin through a moral and imaginative shock which totally disrupts our world. His teaching seeks to give that shock, and the mythological ideas of the coming of God, the destruction of the world order, the reversal of customary social, ritual and ethical systems of grading, and the emergence of the age of salvation provided the appropriate and convenient imagery for the death-and-rebirth of the self, society and the world-order, which was necessary if the reign of God were to be fully realized on earth.

The evidence suggests that Jesus finally completed and resolved Israel's religious history by discovering in his own person and seeking to communicate salvation by faith. The New Testament is unanimous in affirming the priority and importance of John the Baptist here. The Baptist preached the imminence of God's reign, and demanded that the whole nation should undergo a kind of purification rite. Ritual washing, by way of symbolically cleansing oneself in preparation for entering God's presence, is attested at that time in every quarter of Jewish life. In the Baptist's preaching it was a final eschatological purification of the nation in preparation for the reign of God. To a person steeped in the Hebrew Bible it would naturally evoke the promises of the great prophets of old:

> I will sprinkle clean water upon you . . . a new heart I will give you, and a new spirit I will put within you; and I will take out of your flesh the heart of stone and give you a heart of flesh. And I will put my spirit within you . . . (Ezekiel 36:25–27)

If we set aside the later ideas that Jesus was himself divine, sinless and in no need of salvation, the obvious inference from the evidence is that Jesus was deeply impressed by John, willingly and wholeheartedly underwent John's baptism — and received from it far more than John knew he was giving. Jesus experienced the entire devastating reality of salvation by faith, the gift of the divine spirit and the arrival of the kingdom in his own person. He had received in himself the salvation which the whole of Jewish tradition had been eagerly awaiting. John preached one baptism, in preparation for the kingdom, but Jesus received another, baptism *into* it. And so he shortly appeared in Galilee with a message which went a vital stage beyond John's: scripture is fulfilled, the eschatological reign of God is beginning, repent and believe the good news. He was the pioneer of salvation, the first person in whom the perfect relation between Israel and God for which Judaism longed had at last become actual.

The Christian way to salvation is not something introduced from outside by the descent to earth of a God-man, or by the revelation to the early church of the kerygma. It is simply the final salvation which Judaism looked for, first discovered, experienced and preached by Jesus of Nazareth.

Because Jesus was the first to receive salvation his baptism is given in retrospect something of the air of a coronation: it is his commissioning by God to be the Messiah (Mark 1:9–11, evoking Psalm 2:7, 1 Samuel 16:13, and several passages in Isaiah 42, 44, 49 etc.). This is a later and mythological interpretation. But behind the use of such titles as 'Messiah' and 'Son of God' stands the Christian claim that Jesus completed ancient Israel's religious quest by first discovering the true and final way to God and giving it definitive expression in his teaching.

69

Dispensationalist ideas of history are all mythological. There is no demonstrable and divine necessity in the fact that the discovery was made by this particular man at this particular moment. It could conceivably have been another man, at another place and time. But it happened to be this man at this particular time and place. Critical historical study, carried out with sufficient religious sympathy, and covering the Old Testament, inter-testamental and New Testament periods, may seek to show immanently why it makes sense that it should have been among this most religiously gifted of all peoples, at this particular time of acute stress, that a radical Galilean *hasid* should have been the first, the first of all.

The reception of the reign of God through the gift of the divine Spirit in response to faith and repentance is the Christian way to salvation. In its fullest development it promises to bring about the complete transformation of the self, society and the world-order. The content of that future order cannot be described because it is so discontinuous with present reality, but it is projected as the most perfect possible state of affairs, for it is the complete reconciliation of the self, society, the world and God, and in Jesus' message it is promised universally and immediately. Thus Christianity—Jesus' way of salvation—is the final truth, and the society which springs from him, even if it has confused his way, has never wholly lost it. And this, from the critical point of view, is the sense in which Christianity is the absolute religion. It is not an absolute metaphysical theory of the world, but the final project for the world's transformation into perfection.

Something resembling Jesus' way has cropped up independently in the eastern religions, especially in Amida or Pure-Land Buddhism and in some schools of Hinduism. There is no logical difficulty in supposing that the same religious truth may have been discovered by others beside Jesus. All that Christianity need claim is that Jesus' way to God is adequate and final. If others have found it too, so much the better, but I believe that in fact there is no other vision of the highest good as complete as his, and no other way of siezing and enjoying it in advance as powerful as his.

What of the status of Jesus himself? Since his message and outlook was wholly God-centred it would have been quite inappropriate for him to permit any cult of personality or to make claims on his own behalf. The synoptic gospels preserve abundant evidence of his reticence, and critical study has gradually recognized that he did not claim to be a divine being, nor to be the Messiah, nor even perhaps to be the Man or 'Son of Man', the representative human being who receives the kingdom of God. Mark emphasizes this reticence to an extent that was long thought puzzling, though it is very much of a piece with the importance and subtle teaching on secrecy in the practice of religion preserved in Matthew 6. (The material in Matthew 6 may well be secondary, but it is so consistent with a good deal else in the tradition that it is probably congruent with Jesus' own outlook.) In effect, one can only be something before God by being nothing before God: one can only be possessed by God and one cannot possibly possess any status before God, so that the discourse of a man of God cannot possibly be about himself but only about God. Or if he can speak of himself, all that he can speak of is the suffering he must yet undergo till the triumph of God is complete. There is no exception to that fundamental law of the relation to God, and certainly not in the case of Jesus himself, so that the empirical evidence is as we should expect, namely that Jesus' only teaching about himself concerns the suffering that he must undergo.

What is the meaning of this suffering? Certainly not any of the confusing and often morally offensive later Christian doctrines of the atonement. For a being who is flesh to become spirit is not easy. God is overwhelmingly different from man, and the relation to God requires and demands a total renunciation which cannot be without pain. The self-in-its-world must die and pass away utterly if God's new world is to come, and naturally the flesh resists this, for the drive to maintain one's biological life is even more frantic and desperate than the sexual drive. So the coming of the kingdom is opposed violently, and the kingdom-bearer must be at the centre of the storm of opposition. He must bear in his own person the brunt of men's incomprehension, natural mistrust and hatred of the new reality that he brings and the repellent demand that it makes. Like other prophets before him but still more intensely Jesus must suffer the violence of men and interpret it

71

religiously as affliction laid on him by God, the eschatological tribulation through which alone the kingdom can be securely established. And this 'cup' that he must drink is one which his close associates must share with him.

This view of Jesus' death is abundantly present even in the very short list of probably authentic sayings given in the last chapter, so it is surprising that Bultmann should suggest that we do not know how Jesus saw his own death. It is true that Jesus knew nothing of the sacrificial, transactional and legal language in which Christianity subsequently spoke of his death, but he had an entirely intelligible view of his own. Having experienced the power of salvation he did not withdraw into mystical seclusion, but following the Baptist's example attempted a public mission to the nation. For the reign of God was not just an inner experience, but was to be a public and social reality. From the outset this public mission encountered varying degrees of astonishment, incredulity, scepticism, ridicule and open hostility. People's inability to accept the best news there could possibly be seemed to Jesus demonic, and he saw himself as involved in a cosmic conflict whose logical outcome could only be his own death, the price of the kingdom.

In a rather pigheaded and unconscious way the public always tests the courage and persistence of a man of extraordinary vision by its neglect, misunderstanding, mockery and even hatred; and somewhat similarly Jesus was subjected to the trial of faith by his own generation. The available evidence suggests that he consistently interpreted the opposition he met theologically, and fought it so hard as to carry his mission to the symbolic centre of israel's faith at the Temple and so precipitate his own final ordeal. Increasingly clearly, commitment to the proclamation of the kingdom entailed acceptance of his death as a fate laid upon him by God.

It is doubtful whether he can be said to have instituted the Eucharist, but it is likely that at the Last Supper he associated the sharing of the bread and the cup of affliction with his followers' participation in his fate. Sharing his sufferings, they would eventually share in the kingdom-feasting with him, a theme well attested elsewhere in his teaching. And this is all that is needed for a critical Christian understanding of Jesus' death. Jesus' experience of the kingdom and revelation of the way were tested to the end in his own life, the trial of faith that he endured is exemplary and archetypal, and in Christian ritual believers conform themselves to that archetype in order to follow in his way and share in his destiny.

In Christian belief, then, Jesus is the first discoverer, the prophet, the teacher and the exemplar of the perfect way to salvation, and so unique and the central figure in human history. Titles like 'Christ' (Messiah) are mythological, but are permissible as reminders of the historical context in which he appeared and against the background of which he should be understood. It is important not to mistake their meaning: the expression 'Son of God' for example, is a metaphor meaning roughly the same as 'Man of God' in modern English. Jesus was the most-God-revealing man, filled with God's Spirit and in a definitive and exemplary human relation to God; but if the expression begins to be taken any more literally than that, Jesus begins to be distorted and corrupted.

The growth of a kind of confessional rhetoric around Jesus is early and remarkable. Borrowing traditional language about the divine Wisdom, some saw him within twenty years of his death as a pre-existent heavenly figure. This is a very high flight of mythopoeic imagination, but it can be given an intelligible interpretation. Jesus can be called the final cause of creation in the sense that in him the highest good is attained and the world comes to fruition, and he can be called the first-born of all creation in the sense that in him the creature at last enters into its perfect relation to the Creator and the Creator's work is complete. In Jesus the creature at last becomes Spirit, and God is all in all. He anticipated—seized in advance—the end of all things. In that strictly eschatological sense he may be called 'divine', but if his divinity is brought forward into the history of this world and he is seen as bequeathing divine authority to a succession of rulers in church and state, Christianity is destroyed and spritual liberation is exchanged for political subjection. The protestant Reformers, when they set out to dismantle Christendom, saw something of this but not enough, and they completed only half their task. They wanted Christianity to continue to be a system of social control, and so they shrank back from completing the Reformation. Christianity had for so long been understood in terms of the political requirements of Greco-Roman culture that they could not see what it might become if it was to be *wholly* purged of corruption. They knew well enough that the developed traditional dogma was not entirely scriptural, yet they left Protestantism asserting both the sufficiency of scripture and the necessity of the doctrines, an unhappy contradiction, because they did not see clearly how and why they must one day be reformed.

What about Jesus' status and continued life after his death? The oldest faith was simply in the exaltation of Jesus by God, within which eventually a series of stages were distinguished: the resurgence, the appearances of the risen one, the ascension, the heavenly session, the pentecostal gift, the second advent, the millennial reign of Christ, and so on. The differentiation of these stages was linked with the development of a liturgical calendar at first based on and then breaking away from the old Passover and Pentecost. The stages are not events in a biography of Jesus' post-mortem, but mythical projections of faith. The root idea which began their development is that through the crisis brought about by Jesus' death the disciples at last came fully to faith, came that is to a full participation in the salvation which he introduced into the world. Tradition suggests Peter was the first of them. To these early believers Jesus had indeed attained the kingdom, was the Messiah, the firstborn and the Beloved. In him was the epitome or first fruit of the final salvation now beginning. The fullness of the divine Spirit was now poured out not just on him alone, but upon the society of his followers.

Without the mythology, what was and is the risen life of Jesus himself? Mark includes a conflict story which purports to indicate Jesus' own view in 12:18–27. The last two verses (26–27) must probably be discarded and the whole story may be secondary, but at any rate it shows Jesus, though siding with the Pharisees against the Sadducees, being careful to repudiate crude ideas of the resurrection. The comparison with the angels (verse 25) suggests a timeless disembodied life in communion with God. The story is the best indication we have as to what Jesus' own teaching may have been, and it suggests that the saved who are wholly transformed into Spirit exist eternally in God in some indescribable way. The reason

74

for believing in this 'future' state is simply that it can be anticipated in this life.

In the resurrection appearances Jesus is seen 'bodily', but so are angels. The stories are products of the Easter faith rather than reports of physical events which gave rise to it. They are projections of the faith of the early church, the content of which is drawn from traditions of Jesus' earthly life and from the Eucharist. The faith which they express might be summarized thus: 'Participating in the salvation Jesus brought, I know and I know he knew the eternal God, and thus to know God, or rather to be known by God, is to have conquered death. By the power of God which is the Spirit of God he lives in God, and I know that this salvation will grow until it encompasses all things.'

4

GOD

God the Saviour

An incarnate god would surely be expected to speak in a direct oracular manner, so that his utterance would draw people to the mystery of his own person and lead them to worship him. The idea that Jesus was such a being often leads people to understand his words in that way, and they find in John's gospel one who does indeed speak rather as if he were an incarnate god. So if my account of the message of the real Jesus is anywhere near the mark in stressing its indirect character and its cunning stratagems, then Jesus' own teaching-style is a strong argument against an incarnational interpretation of him. It is hard to see any possible meaning for the common expression 'Jesus is God' which is compatible with the character and content of his message. He will not permit us to deify the man or to humanize the Deity, though many people wish to do one or the other. One cannot say Jesus is the only God there is, and one cannot say Jesus is another God alongside the one God.

For those who still wish to affirm the divinity of Christ there is no other solution except one along the lines laid down at the Council of Chalcedon. First one must distinguish co-equal persons within the unity of the divine nature, and secondly one must suppose that in what appears to be a human being one of these divine persons has replaced the human person. Thus a full human nature has been annexed to a divine person.

To realize imaginatively what Chalcedon says is very difficult, but here is the closest possible parallel case. Imagine a human who from the moment of his first conception has been taken over by an immensely powerful alien intelligence. For reasons of its own the alien does not wish to swamp him

76

entirely, so it permits him to enjoy a relatively autonomous human intelligence and will; but he is not really an individual human being. He is the alien living a fully human life.

It will immediately be objected that this analogy is prejudicial for it compares the incarnation with certain science-fiction nightmares. This is true; but if it be insisted that Jesus' relation to God is quite different in kind from ours then it is hard to see how the comparison can be avoided. Orthodoxy had to say that Jesus' humanity was 'impersonal'.

Still the argument persists that because Jesus is the saviour, Jesus is God. From the critical point of view the starting-point must be Jesus' words. Yes, they are saving, and he did show the true and final way to salvation: it is to give up everything including our own righteousness and even our own lives and trust wholly in the coming of God. Jesus lived his own way, even to death, and those who hear his words and identify themselves with him in his way experience his salvation. So, as one who follows his way and has tasted his salvation, I call him saviour. For me he is the Way.

So far, this may be clear enough and sufficient. But Christendom went on to produce very elaborate doctrines and arguments about the mechanism of salvation, which are claimed to require a much more developed theology. Are they valid, and do they require it?

Christendom Christianity elevated Jesus to a cosmic status very like that of ancient kings. He was the universal monarch, and the mediator between the heavenly and earthly realms. He bound the cosmos together, and all authority in church and state descended from him. There was some biblical warrant for all this, for in Israel too there had been for a time a throne-and-altar synthesis, with the king as the Son of God or God's earthly viceroy. Jesus was the expected messianic king, and his domain was universal. He was enthroned in heaven. So the old Israelite royal psalms were transferred to him as Christ Almighty.

This developed theology effectively claims that eschatological hope has been realized in the present age. The Byzantine theocracy is the kingdom of God, over which Christ rules as king. In the Byzantine emperor's palace there was a throne for Christ with a gospel book lying on it.

The doctrine of Christ's co-equal divinity tightened up the authority of the whole system. Jesus was believed to have given plenary authority to the church. So if Jesus himself was co-equally divine, then his authority was absolute, and the authority of those who acted in his name was absolute.

The fourth-century Greek Fathers developed Christendom's single most important theological argument in support of this new system. It runs as follows:

1. Salvation is the union of man with God.
2. Through its faith and its rites the church offers salvation to its members.
3. The Saviour who unites believers with God is Jesus Christ and him alone.
4. Christ cannot unite us with or communicate to us what he does not himself possess, so he must have in himself the fullness of the divine nature.
5. If Christ unites the human believer entire with God, then he must also possess the fullness of human nature.
6. Therefore Christ the Saviour must be perfect God and perfect Man (the two-natures doctrine).
7. To fulfill his uniting function he must himself be one person; and since this union is a divine act that person must be a divine person, the person of God's co-equal, co-eternal Word.
8. Does he, in lacking a human person (7), lack the fullness of human nature (5)? No, for he has a human soul and [it was later added] a human will, and so is capable of experiencing the suffering and temptation described in the gospels.

This Greek argument is strongly cosmological in its concerns. At one pole in the cosmic scale stands the eternal, holy and incorruptible deity, and at the other pole is frail, sinful man in time. Salvation is a seemingly impossible union of the two, and yet it is real, for the church gives it. So the principle of salvation must be a being which unites the opposites and is both divine and human without confusion. Salvation is incorporation into this being.

The argument effectively binds together the power of the church, the cosmic Christ and salvation. But it is markedly deductive, for all it really presupposes is the definitions of God and man and the claim that in the church their union is accomplished. The part played in it by Jesus is minimal, except as an historical anchor and as the source of a slight embarrassment (8). Salvation is accomplished by the incarnation, the union of the two natures.

Now there was also in Christendom, particularly in the west, a tradition that regarded Jesus' death as the hinge on which our salvation turns. If this is so then the Greek argument is insufficient. Anselm of Canterbury gave classic expression to the western point of view. His theory is as deductive as the Greek one, for it starts from definitions of God, man, sin and salvation, from which Anselm proves that God lay under a moral necessity to secure man's salvation by sending into the world a God-man to die an innocent sacrificial death for our sakes. The main steps are these:

1. Salvation is union with God.
2. God destines man for salvation.
3. God is infinite in justice and mercy.
4. Man owes God a debt of perfect service.
5. Man has sinned, witholding God's due.
6. This sin is of infinite gravity, and merits damnation.
7. Man must make voluntary reparation to God.
8. But he cannot, for sin has weakened his will, and in any case an infinite satisfaction is needed to right an infinite wrong.
9. So man cannot attain salvation (4–8).
10. God's justice requires man's condemnation, while yet the eternal purpose of his mercy is to grant man salvation (2, 3, 6).
11. If there is a solution to this conflict God will be morally bound to adopt it (3).
12. The solution is the incarnation and obedience even to death of the God-man Jesus Christ. For:
13. The Saviour must be man, to make satisfaction for man (7).
14. The Saviour must be God, that his act may have infinite worth (8).
15. He must live a perfect human life and voluntarily die an utterly ignominious and undeserved death in perfect obedience to God, so that his act may acquire infinite merit in God's sight.

16. God owes him a reward, but he desires nothing for himself; so he is most fittingly rewarded by the transfer of his merit and the gift of salvation to those for whose sake he offered his supreme sacrifice.

17. Thus in him man gives God what is due (4) and attains salvation (2), and God's mercy and justice are upheld and indeed shown to be one (3).

The Greek argument and Anselm's argument are only two of many eastern and western arguments which seek to show how man's salvation has been objectively accomplished, and that Jesus Christ the Saviour must because of the nature of his act be in the fullest sense a divine being.

But all such theories have a difficulty in them. In biblical and all other kinds of monotheistic faith it is impossible to regard salvation as a work performed upon God. God may act to save through a human instrument, but the one God is the only Saviour, and salvation is immediate union with God.

Theories of the work of Christ confuse this principle. In order to show Jesus' distinct divinity they represent salvation as a work done by Jesus with the object of uniting the human being with God, or propitiating God, or draining God's wrath, or offering God a gift. This work done by Jesus objectively changes the relationship between man and God, and since it is a saving work, and salvation is a most purely divine work, then Jesus must be co-equally divine. One stage of the argument requires a separation of Christ's saving work from God, and another admits that salvation cannot be so separated. And in all their forms such arguments end by establishing a new and complex system of religious meditation.

The Bible in general, and Jesus in particular, point to an end-state of perfect religious immediacy; but Christendom became as complex a system of religious mediation as the Old Covenant had been. Something had gone wrong with the notion of mediation. In Christendom Jesus Christ came to stand between man and God, so that God looks through Jesus to see man, and from the opposite side man looks through Jesus to see what God is like. But Jesus himself was a mediator in a different sense. He stood aside a little, in order to bring about a direct head-on collision between man and the pure

80

godness of God, a collision he himself also had to endure. For him salvation could only be found in that encounter. He effects the introduction, but has no intention of interposing himself between the parties. For him, God alone is the Saviour, and only when we have that point clear will we have a sound basis on which to think about his work.

This is not to say that the work of Jesus is as self-effacing as the work of John the Baptist. On the contrary, it is highly significant that of all the great founders of religions Jesus is the most troubled and disturbing. The gospel tradition as it developed tended to play down the evidence of his turbulent and restless temperament, in the interest of showing him to Christians as a model of calm endurance of persecution. But even in John's gospel, where the process of stylization has well-nigh effaced the historical Jesus, traces of distress, anger and inner turmoil remain. In the synoptic gospels the conflict begins with Jesus' baptism and ceases only with his death.

We have suggested that in Jesus' thought there is a union of Wisdom and eschatological elements. The relation to God is at once inner experience and cosmic event. Inwardly, Jesus' affliction is the *peirasmos* or trial of faith mentioned in the temptation narratives and in the Lord's Prayer, but it is also projected outwards mythologically as the 'messianic woes', the terrible time of cosmic anarchy, affliction and persecution which must be endured before the victory of God is complete. This theme of suffering both inner and cosmic is clearly linked with other themes such as the battle against evil powers, the collision of worlds and the great reversal. The one who imposes the affliction is seen sometimes as God, sometimes as Satan.

All this may seem obscure and remote, but it is not so. One who has endured religious suffering knows perfectly well what it is to be in a state where inner suffering has cosmic significance, and one does not know whether it is God or Satan with whom one struggles. The exoticism and strangeness of Jesus' ideas is only superficial. The evidence we have suggests that he himself underwent this experience throughout the period of his public life, that it figured prominently in his teaching, that he thought it an inescapable stage in the realization of the kingdom of God, that he saw his death as its culmination, and that he sought to associate his disciples with himself in it. He did not think of himself as suffering *instead* of others, but rather regarded the final tribulation as a general principle of the relation to God. He above all had to endure the confrontation to which he led others, he was at the centre of the storm; but his followers must join him there if they too were to break through to the kingdom. Too much emphasis on the divinity of his person and the vicarious or substitutionary character of his work can only obscure the truth that his experience must be shared by his followers. And his death does not have saving efficacy of itself, by the mere carnal fact of being a death, but only as setting the seal upon his life and teaching. Natural death is subordinate to the infinitely more important religious death of the self which the relation to God requires. This religious death of the self is brought about by moral and sacramental union with Jesus in his trial of faith, his death and resurrection. Jesus' way to God is enacted ritually in the Christian sacraments. It is both a once-for-all victory and a continual process as the self moves through time in faith.

God Transcendent

Here is a very strange sequence of events. In the book of Genesis God is portrayed as setting up the cosmic order and expressing satisfaction with it. It is to be the permanent divinely ordained framework for human life. Then in the gospels Jesus appears declaring that the world is under the dominion of Satan and prophesying in the name of God the overthrow of the very order that God has established. But a few centuries later Jesus—now transformed into the enthroned Christ Almighty of the Christian empire—is found presiding over a reconstituted cosmic order of greater elaboration than ever. A whole series of heavens stretches up to the divine throne, and a corresponding series of hells beneath dives down to Satan in the lowest pit. Finally, time's pendulum swings back, the great Christendom cosmology passes away, and Jesus again begins to be seen as a human figure concerned only with salvation, the prophet of the kingdom of God. The primitive eschatological faith begins to return, and to displace the developed dogmatic faith.

82

Something analogous can be seen in the case of Buddhism. In a world in which elaborate sacred cosmologies were common the Buddha is said to have told his disciples that cosmology and even theology were topics of no real religious interest, and they should attend exclusively to spirituality. Yet when Buddhism became the basic faith of whole societies the Buddha himself was made the pivot of elaborate cosmological systems. In time those systems passed away and are now no more than intriguing curiosities, but the original message of the Buddha (so far as it can be discerned) is still challenging.

It seems that to those very rare figures who are truly religious the metaphysical and cosmological side of religion is a distraction and an irrelevance, something to be avoided. But society has a persistent need and desire for a sacred cosmological framework to live in, and is quite capable of building one around a man whose whole message was a warning against such things. Of course something of the teaching of Jesus and of Buddha was incorporated into these developed cosmological systems, but the incongruity is nevertheless obvious, and particularly so in the case of Jesus. In developed dogmatic Christianity the ways people think about God and Jesus are pervasively influenced by the desire to affirm order, authority and stability in the cosmos and society. Hence the emphasis on cosmic rank, correct doctrine, divine authority and due obedience.

Christendom is all but gone, and we can now see how different the emperor Constantine's cosmic Christ was from the real Jesus. The divine Christ of Christendom is an obstacle to the recovery of the real Jesus and his message, and the spiritual renewal of Christianity demands a break with deeply engrained habits of thought. From the purely religious point of view the human Jesus who speaks not of himself but of God is a far greater figure than Christendom's cosmic overlord.

A corresponding purification is also necessary in the case of God. The religious imagination is constantly dragging God down to the human level, envisaging God as masculine so that men may rule women as God rules nature, as a lawgiver who promulgates and enforces the moral law as legislators and judges do the civil law, as an Emperor of emperors who rules all nations, and as an undying all-observing Father from

83

whose watchful and censorious eye we can never escape.

But if this tendency is unchecked religion becomes so objectified as to be a tyranny which does not allow the free individual human spirit to emerge at all. In the great Bronze-Age cities the outcome was a slave society. The cosmos and the city were constructed by the gods for themselves to inhabit, and human beings were insignificant serfs of the gods. Ancient Egypt has left us the names of far more gods than men, and the gods are much more vivid characters than men. If perchance a man's gifts and achievements were such that he could not but be remembered, the conclusion was drawn that he must in that case be not a man but a god.

How was the individual human being to assert himself in the face of such a crushing weight of divinity? It was done by asserting a wholly new and greater dimension of religion. City religion was objectified, public and cosmological, but the new movement was iconoclastic, inward and spiritual. The old concern was for creation and a stable public divine order, whereas the new concern was for redemption from an evil, transient and idolatrous world.

Thus the emergence of faith in the Transcendent coincides with and is indeed identical with the emergence of the individual human spirit. Where it is grasped that God is Spirit then man has become spirit.

The ancient task of religion had been to bind society together and ground the moral order in the natural order. So it generated a public system of sacred images, the God of social religion, who was expressed in and bound to the cosmos and society. But the prophets declared that the true God is not identical with this public covenanted order and not bound by it. God may choose to destroy it, may defeat and scatter the holy people and may abrogate the entire ritual system. For God is invisible and free and may not be bound by any system of images. And in so far as the individual can understand and say this, then he has become spirit as God is Spirit. He has become a unique individual, set aside from the womb for his particular destiny. Filled with the divine Spirit, he has authority to judge public religion.

The God of public religion, God in symbolic representation, is embedded in a particular conceptual apparatus through

84

which society and the world are seen. But the true God who is Spirit calls man to transcend that apparatus and to participate in God's own pure freedom and creativity. This destiny should not be seen as reserved for a tiny minority of charismatic heroes of faith. Israel looked for a time when *all* the Lord's people would be prophets, nobody would be taught to know God by his neighbour, and the divine Spirit would be poured out on all.

Since no actual religious order can content the spirit, religious hope is eschatological. The ideal is always ahead. It is the kingdom of God, a projected perfect synthesis of the cosmic, social and individual aspects of religion. It is a state of general salvation in which every individual, being filled with the divine Spirit, is fulfilled as free individual spirit; it is a perfect society without ranking or mediation because every individual is immediately related to God; and it is a perfected and renewed world. Jesus' proclamation and revelation of the kingdom of God is therefore the most comprehensive and final religious message there can be. His teaching is the final religious truth and the final hope.

However, one cannot identify any particular historical state of Christianity as the final religion. Historical religion is imperfect and transient, and is kept living by self-criticism and eschatological hope.

The consequence of all this for faith in God is that pure faith is a continual struggle against anthropomorphism, objectification and the tyranny they create. It is certainly possible to go too far in one's insistence upon the divine transcendence and fall into an excess of enthusiasm like that of the gnostic Basilides, who described God as 'not even indescribable' (cited by G. C. Stead, *Divine Substance,* Oxford University Press 1977, page 159)! But I believe that one must nonetheless affirm that 'God' is non-objective, though I must hasten to add what I do and do not mean by this.

A great deal of our talk about God and our argument about the existence of God goes upon the assumption that one can first define what is meant by the word 'God', and then decide whether there is in fact a being answering to that description. First one frames a specification for God, and then one asks if there is something that meets this specification.

But the main tradition of belief in God has always insisted that God is infinite, simple, indescribable and absolute (that is, not essentially related to anything other than God). If that is so, how can any specification of God which can be sure of picking out God ever be framed? Many people think that God can be specified relationally by saying that if a thing is creator of the world then that thing must be God, but the creator of the world may not be God. Marcion, a second-century writer, denied that the creator was God, and though he may have been wrong he was not obviously uttering a self-contradiction.

The point is that as soon as one fixes any definite idea of God[1], the possibility immediately arises that there might be a God[2], surpassing God[1]. But in that case God[2] must be the true God and God[1] must be an idol, for it is certainly essential to the notion of faith that the God in whom it believes is unsurpassable.

If this is true then faith in God cannot be propositional belief, belief via a concept, belief that a certain understood specification is in fact fulfilled. Instead of seeing faith as assent to the proposition that a certain definite individual object exists, we have to see it as a continually moving aspiration after that which does not permit itself to be grasped as a definite object. If faith projects a representation of its object it may do so only in the knowledge that such a projected representation is provisional and imperfect. Living faith in a transcendent God requires that one be continually willing to renounce one's provisional notion of God, for whatever that notion may be God surpasses it.

Thus one cannot have faith in the true God via a concept; one can only believe directly, by faith's receptivity to the transcendent. God can only be defined *in relation to faith*, as that which alone deserves worship, that which is the object of the purest and most perfect faith. The dogmatic habit of mind attempts to fix the object of faith, but as soon as it succeeds in doing so faith dies. Faith must as it were have a variable focus, so that there can be movement in the religious life in response to a God who is changelessly transcendent. The God of dogmatic and metaphysical belief is an idol people cling to: the true God is always ahead and is apprehended practically and ascetically

86

by a continuing act of renunciation through which one moves forward. The existence of God can only be shown indirectly by showing faith's continual movement, its critical character, its receptivity and the sovereign freedom of the spiritual liberation it enjoys. It is from this continual movement forward that theism gains its historical impetus.

Hence the intensely practical character of Jesus' teaching. Unconcerned with speculation of any kind, his legacy is a body of highly charged words, linguistic actions which incite us to act in faith: to renounce, to decide, to step forward into the reign of God. In pressing to the limit the themes of God's holiness and transcendence, God's nearness in absolute demand and God's confounding gift of salvation, Jesus anticipated the goal of the life of faith, the end of the world. He taught and enacted the reign of God, a way of living as spirit by the power of the divine Spirit so that divine justice, love and forgiveness are expressed immediately and without loss in the way human beings behave towards each other. In such a world each human being is as God to each other human being. The God of Jesus is God absolutely because of Jesus' perfect proclamation of the kingdom of God, his seizure and enactment of the final state of the world in which faith finds its consummation.

The Way to God

What is the relation between religious and historical action? To many people it has seemed obvious that religious commitment demands an ascetical withdrawal from active life in the world. In the historical sphere of existence there is no unchanging and unmixed good, but only ambiguity and relativity. The more involved in it one becomes by the way of family life, ownership of possessions, membership of institutions or political action, the more aware one is of enmeshment in compromise. It is true that in the present century it has been widely urged that man exists only for society and for history and that an eternal religious concern is not an authentic possibility, but there are many signs of revolt against this doctrine. For to say that man exists only for society and for history seems to amount in practice to saying that he exists only for

87

the state, and the available pictures of a wholly secular human future are so dismal that people may well turn again to asceticism.

The ascetic says that to find what is perfect and eternal one must entirely renounce active life in the world and the illusory passions that drive it. There must be the utmost simplicity and austerity in one's outer and inner life. The greedy, despairing and defensive ego which is created by life in the world is death and must be put to death. Renouncing all one's former ways of thinking, acting and feeling, one moves towards perfect inner stillness and emptiness. The ultimate goal is to become the *tathagata,* the one who has gone and is no more.

Clearly the ascetic saint who has reached such a state cannot return to history and has no message for those who still live in history. His only ethical prescription is, 'Do no harm to anything,' which in a corrupt world amounts to a command to do nothing. So in the contrast between a Marxist and a Jain saint one can see the antithesis between historical and religious striving in its most extreme form.

Now the monotheistic faiths have believed that they escape this antinomy. They have inherited from the Jews a belief in an historical revelation, historical providence and historical salvation. The ordinary believer living in history has thought that he could please God and relate himself to God by active striving in collaboration with God's historical providence. Because God governs the course of history the active virtues have eternal worth.

But this confidence is based upon a theology of history, a theology which gives a special status to my own society and its tradition. My people, it is implied, are a chosen people who have been singled out to receive a special revelation and perform a unique historical mission. So we alone know God's proper Name. The way we understand God's will and serve God is definitive and all others are unbelievers. Our history is privileged and we have a guarantee of indefectibility, for through our history runs a thread of divine continuity which cannot be broken.

There is no doubt that these convictions have given the monotheistic faiths great strength as creators of enduring communities. But they are open to an obvious objection: there

88

are many such faiths, so what is one to say when they conflict with each other? It begins to look as if the claims that one book is a unique revelation of God and one society occupies a unique position in God's historical design are merely sectarian. Universal spiritual monotheism is reduced to a number of conflicting tribal henotheisms, each claiming that the God of its venerated founder-figure is the only true God.

What happens when God is bound to the history of one particular community can be shown by analysing what happens to the word 'God' when it is used possessively. A god is something which is the object of a religious attitude, and a particular named God is that to which a particular society's form of faith points. That god is *their* God. My God is the object of my faith, and your God of yours. How then can we establish that my God is identical with your God? By the appeal to history, for if my God is the God of Abraham and your God is the God of Abraham then your God and my God are one and the same, and we are brothers.

In this way the identity of a particular deity becomes a social and historical question. If a peacemaker were attempting to draw Jews, Christians and Muslims together, he would have to proceed by arguing that the God of Christians is the Father of Jesus Christ, and the God of Jesus was the God of the Patriarchs; and similarly the God of Islam is the God of Muhammad, who is also ultimately the God of Abraham. In the real world of men there are no free-floating deities, for *all* gods are covenanted to the histories of particular societies.

Christianity is no exception to the rule. Suppose that the absoluteness of Jesus be affirmed by declaring him to be unique incarnation of deity in time, and by claiming that the church is infallible and indefectible. The result is the creation of a Christian god alongside all the other tribal gods. In each case the particular deity is defined in terms of that particular society's form of faith, its claim to the unconditional allegiance of it members, and its historical continuity.

Living as we do in a multi-faith world, where everyone is aware of sectarian conflict and rivalry between different religious communities, it is not surprising that traditional monotheistic faith in the religious value of the active life of historical struggle has been seriously undermined. How can

89

you be quite sure that to give your life to the service of one particular historical society is to perform an action of eternal religious value? In spite of all the rhetoric to the contrary, we cannot now believe that those who died for England on the battlefront in 1916 gave their lives as an offering acceptable to God. Even missionaries are not as certain as they were that to destroy an ancient tribal culture by evangelism and westernization is unquestionably right.

In various ways people have tried to overcome the difficulty by seeking a truly universal God beyond the all-too-human gods of the historical religions. The English *deists* sought a purely philosophical essence of religion, independent of any particular historical society. The *idealists,* following Hegel, tried to compass in thought the movement of world history as a whole and discern its emerging total religious meaning. *Syncretism,* exemplified in our time by John Hick's planetary system of faiths revolving around the one divine Reality, suggests that there are many possible paths to God. A global theology of religions might draw on the insights of many faiths in the hope of formulating a universal spirituality and ethic for the future. Finally, *Arthur Schopenhauer* was led to something like the ascetic's pessimism and withdrawal from history with which we began.

In their different ways all these four solutions have given up the traditional Christian claim that outside the church there is no salvation because Jesus is the final truth for the whole human race.

There is one solution which does maintain the old claim, but only at the price of almost removing Christianity from history. It is put forward by *Søren Kierkegaard* in some, but not all of his writings. On this view the essential Christian belief is that there has been one utterly paradoxical embodiment of the eternal in time in the incarnation, which is apprehended afresh each time an individual person believes. But Kierkegaard denies that the historically conditioned details of Jesus' life are of ultimate religious interest, and he denies the traditional Roman Catholic and Orthodox belief that the substance of Christianity is permanently embodied and transmitted in history in the form of the church. We cannot make an absolute out of the contingent facts of Jesus' life, nor out of the histori-

90

cal tradition of the church. The substance of Christianity exists only in a string of occasional miracles, moments when individuals believe and lay hold of it.

In order to protect Christianity from being debased and dissolved away by historical relativity Kierkegaard is forced virtually to take it out of history altogether. His heroic individualism and inwardness show how deeply he took to heart the problem raised by the critical view of history. But he only partly saves Christianity. His authoritarian and irrational view of the incarnation does not do justice to Jesus, and his intense inwardness makes it hard to see how there can be any visible church, or even any visibly Christian ethic lived by the believer in history. Christianity can only be a history-transcending secret which cannot become publicly and historically visible.

The solution to which our argument has been pointing is not quite the same as any of these five. If we set aside the developed this-worldly dogmatic faith and recall the primitive faith, then we can see that what links Christianity to history is eschatological hope. What is universal and absolute in Christianity is not the tradition which is behind us, but the hope which is ahead of us, not the church but the kingdom of God.

The mission of the Baptist and Jesus was a public mission to the nation, and the kingdom of God was a social reality, not an individual mystical state. To enter it man living in history had to take a decisive ethical step forward in repentance and faith. He answered God's call by breaking with the past and entering upon a wholly new quality of life in which love, forgiveness and mercy were to be shown in a new intensity and purity. And all this emphasis on the public and practical character of Jesus' way to God makes it clear that there must be a church. The Way exists in the world not simply as a possibility for occasional solitary individuals, but in a permanent community that struggles, however imperfectly, to walk in it. But a church that is the prisoner of its own past is not in the Way at all, for the Way is precisely freedom from the past. When Augustine wrote into his theology the church's advance through history he prepared the way for a kind of triumphalism and pride in its own tradition which is now extraordinarily difficult

91

for the older churches to throw off, though the Reformation surely showed that an assault upon the tyranny of the past is a prerequisite for religious renewal. Perhaps it may help us to throw off the past if we recall what was said earlier, that the historical Jesus is a greater and more universal figure than the church's divine Christ. The divine Christ is tied to one particular historical tradition and cannot move people unless they come to stand in that tradition, whereas Jesus has exercised a considerable influence, on India for example, quite beyond the reach of the church. His call to die to the old self and its world and by receiving the Spirit to become a new self in a new world can be heard in any social world, and its force is the same. For it is always true that man is flesh and not spirit, that we construct our world in a series of concentric circles about ourselves, and that we estimate things in terms of their utility in maintaining a fundamentally false and futile construction of ourselves. Jesus' call to escape from all that by a once-for-all decision and receive God's new world is everywhere equally intelligible, alarming and liberating.

To throw off the legacy of Christendom, however, and return to the teaching of Jesus and the primitive faith requires not only that we rescue Jesus from dogmatic captivity, but that we rescue God from metaphysical captivity. The earliest faith was practical and purely religious in its categories, but Christianity gradually became so extensively permeated with dogmatic, philosophical and cosmological ways of thinking that by now many people find it hard to recognize the purely religious as a category at all. Thus in our talk of God the non-religious God of the philosophers has held the field more or less continuously since the thirteenth century, and in spite of numerous valiant attempts a truly religious understanding of God has not yet been restored to general currency.

If Jesus is the way to God, then our understanding of what is meant by 'God' must be conformed to the manner of his speaking about God and the nature of the decision for which he calls. Jesus does not teach a theology, list the divine attributes, prove God's existence or define God. But it is possible to speak of rules for the use of the word 'God'. They are five in number:

92

1. It is possible to say what God is not, for to answer God one must repudiate all that is not God.
2. One may seek to show what God is by special linguistic techniques, such as those used by Jesus.
3. One may speak of God in traditionally authorized ways, using an image coupled with an adjective such as eternal, heavenly, almighty, or everlasting. The resulting phrases are, as H. L. Mansel (in *The Limits of Religious Thought Examined,* 1858, Lecture 5) would say, 'regulatively true': that is, their force is purely practical. One calls God a 'heavenly Father' because it is right to rely utterly upon God.
4. One may use special technical terms in connection with God which express qualities of the new life in God, such as salvation, grace and forgiveness. Their meaning is apprehended practically.
5. Finally, to learn to use rules 1–4 correctly itself requires a religious discipline.

In a word, to know what God is one must decide for God. There is no benign, all-endorsing, undemanding deity who is satisfied with us and the world as we are, and asks no more of us than loyalty to the received tradition. The one whom Jesus shows demands all that we are and gives all that God is. Even if you stand in the religious tradition and have learnt its language, Jesus still insists that the true God comes as a total surprise.

And the primitive Christian faith, if and when we rediscover it, will also come as a total surprise. What we need today is not the transposition of the remains of Christendom into some liberal or humanist framework of ideas, but something more drastic, a reaffirmation of the purely religious categories in which Christianity first came into the world.

When at the time of the Reformation the New Testament was read afresh it created a great movement of renewal. But today Protestantism is mostly sunk in conservative pietism, and the modern critical reading of the New Testament has not yet brought about a revival of faith. People still feel that it has created more problems than it has solved, and there is an almost palpable longing for renewal coupled with uncertainty and anxiety about what it might involve.

I have suggested that the most obvious starting-point is the bizarre and quite unsatisfactory relationship of developed Christianity to Jesus. If we set aside the vast decaying superstructure of the later dogmatic faith and start with his message, we shall at least have some excuse for continuing to use his name, and more than that, a whole series of themes will begin to be intelligible: the fulfilment of prophetic monotheism, the way to salvation by a final encounter with God, Jesus' death as the consummation of his life's work, identification with Jesus in his way so that he is found himself to be the Way, and the ardent faith of the first Christians who called him Messiah, Lord and Son of God.

WORKING NOTES

Instead of the usual notes and booklists I offer some brief 'working notes' on the main themes of this book, which may help to make them more accessible.

God. The true God is the God of the prophets and of the old tradition of the Negative Way in theology, of which Moses Maimonides (*Guide for the Perplexed,* 1190) is a typical late exponent. Later, what with the influence of Aristotle, growing confidence in secular reason and a certain loss of the old sense of the holy, Christendom's God became objectified.

Very powerful criticisms of this objectified Transcendent were advanced, first by Kant and then by several of the long line of his successors, including Fichte, Hegel, D. F. Strauss and Feuerbach. They mostly took up some mixture of immanentism, humanism and materialism, but the alternative was and still remains a rigorous purification of the concept of God and a return to the older tradition.

Nobody has yet carried out this programme entirely sucessfully, though moves in the right general direction have been made by a variety of neo-Kantians (e.g. H. L. Mansel, *The Limits of Religious Thought Examined,* 1858), existentialists (e.g. R. Bultmann, in several of his essays) and others. The English-speaking world has been slow to learn the lessons of nineteenth-century philosophy, and remains obstinately attached to the God of the period from Aquinas to William Paley.

Linguistic action. The older Liberals, fighting for freedom of expression, drew too sharp a distinction between words and deeds (e.g. J. S. Mill, *On Liberty,* 1859). Philosophers now recognize the great extent to which words, especially spoken words, are used to perform actions. Key names include L. Wittgenstein, J. L. Austin, and J. R. Searle.

In the German tradition people have come to a similar realization by a quite different route: the power of speech in ancient culture was stressed by scholars, and was emphasized by Martin Heidegger; and the Lutheran tradition in preaching was receptive to such ideas.

Jesus' linguistic action. With such a view of God as I hold, religious language appropriately takes the form of revelatory rhetorical devices which jolt us into self-transcendence in response to the presence and call of the Transcendent. That Jesus' preaching is of this kind is beginning to be more clearly understood. The literature is large, but in addition to the books mentioned earlier we may cite Ernst Fuchs, *Studies of the Historical Jesus* (SCM Press 1964); Eta Linnemann, *Parables of Jesus* (SPCK 1966); Joachim Jeremias, *The Parables of Jesus* (SCM Press 1963); Amos Wilder, *Early Christian Rhetoric* (SCM Press 1974); and E. Jüngel's writings.

The older ways of talking about the work of Christ are now largely unintelligible. But Jesus' linguistic action is a work which is still going on, and can directly affect us if we 'hear' it. Hence his teaching work will be central to any future non-mythological doctrine of him, because it is the only non-illusory way to know him.

The historical Jesus. What most Christians describe as the gospel is in my view merely the epistle—secondary affirmations about Jesus rather than the encounter with God through the action of his voice.

But mainstream New Testament scholarship insists that the New Testament is effectively all epistle and no gospel. Even in the synoptics, the evangelists are said to present not so much Jesus as their own 'Christologies': Matthew's so-called gospel is really Matthew's theological epistle.

Faced with so powerfully argued a consensus, and lacking the technical expertise to challenge it, I have been very cautious. For Jesus' life and character, I have scarcely gone beyond the tiny stock of traditions about him which are common to the New Testament as a whole, being attested in the Acts, Paul and Hebrews as well as in the gospels. For Jesus' message, my argument does not depend upon any claim that we can confi-

96

dently identify authentic words *(ipsissima verba)*. Instead, by the use of religious imagination I try to hear and grasp the religious values implicit in the best-attested *general* themes and linguistic forms of his message. To take up Jeremias' useful distinction, I am trying to discern the voice *(ipsissima vox)* rather than select the words.

An analogy from the world of painting may make the point clearer. The Rubens *corpus* doubtless includes a great deal of work by apprentices, employees, continuators, copyists and downright forgers, and we will never know for sure exactly which canvases and passages are really from his own hand. But the man's artistic personality remains accessible. The *vox* remains, even though the *verba* are adulterated. In earlier times it was quite normal for disciples and continuators to go on elaborating a master's *opus* (lifework), and it never occurred to them that in so doing they might obscure the *vox*.

In Jesus' case the *vox* is a highly distinctive form of religious action. Its function is not to express anything about Jesus himself, but to relate the hearer to God. To hear it we must use the appropriate experimental-religious form of listening, and we must listen for a *vox* that is individual, coherent and forcible. What I have so heard, I have reported.

Warm and cold. The traditional Christian stereotype pictured a tender Jesus against the background of a tough Judaism. This stereotype depended upon an odd reading of Jesus and on misrepresentation of his contemporaries. But a day or two with the *Talmud* will show that if you want a warmly intimate piety, regularity and fervour in prayer, a generously mild and liberal ethic, and easy domestic fellowship with a loving and merciful God you would do better to go to the rabbis than to Jesus.

I first met this point years ago in Walter Kaufmann (*Critique of Religion and Philosophy*, Harper and Row 1958, §§ 54, 64–68 etc.). He is heretical and Jewish enough to contrast the liberalism of the rabbis with the severity of Jesus, to point out that intimate piety is typically Jewish not Christian, and to add for good measure that such piety can survive only when artificially sheltered in the family or the ghetto, because it does not stand up well to Socratic questioning in the market-place.

That is a good deal for Christians to swallow, but it is illuminating, and it warns us against too easy an alliance between liberal Protestantism and Reform Judaism on the basis of a liberal Jesus. The gospels suggest a figure not at all like Gamaliel but in the older and sterner school of the prophets, and the *vox* is as tough as Elijah's.

Eschatology. Throughout the critical period the eschatological strain in Jesus and early Christianity has preoccupied theologians. For men like Strauss, Weiss, Schweitzer and the Englishman R. H. Charles it had, indeed, the horrid fascination of an impassable barrier.

More recently there have been attempts to interpret and appropriate it by existentialist theology (R. Bultmann), by the theology of hope (J. Moltmann), and by various forms of radical third-world theology (anthologized by Alistar Kee in *A Reader in Political Theology*, SCM Press 1974). It has even been given a purely secular humanist interpretation (Milan Mahovec, *A Marxist looks at Jesus*, Darton, Longman and Todd 1976), and some have internalized it and explained it in terms of the psychology of conversion. Far from being a blank wall, the primitive eschatology now seems highly flexible and capable of almost too many styles of interpretation. I have sought a purely religious view of eschatology, in line with my emphasis on prophetic monotheism.

Cultural change. Dr. Dennis Nineham (e.g. *The Use and Abuse of the Bible*, Macmillan 1976), in the tradition of Ernst Troeltsch (*The Absoluteness of Christianity*, 1902; Eng. trans. SCM Press 1972), persistently emphasizes the limits of historical knowledge and the fact of cultural change. He will say, I suspect, that the purely religious as a category is just as much historically conditioned as is the secondary superstructure of myth and dogma erected upon it, and he will add that my programme of going back in search of a supposed primitive purity is itself mythological and pre-critical in its assumptions.

Nevertheless, I believe that it is urgently necessary to re-affirm prophetic monotheism, and to make Christianity more coherent with Jesus. To meet Nineham's criticisms I have had to discard as religiously irrelevant the whole obsolete super-
98

natural apparatus of the gospels, and confine myself to the 'voice' of Jesus which reveals the Transcendent. I have had to purify the concept of the religious severely in order to find in Jesus a way of pointing beyond history which is not eroded by the passage of the centuries.

The old problem of the incarnation was, 'How can God enter history and yet remain God?' So phrased, the question is no longer interesting. I rephrase it as, 'How can Jesus' voice be determinative for our relation to God today?' I have offered an answer, but have trodden a very narrow path between Nineham's criticisms on the one hand, and mere emptiness on the other.

The problem is to state Christianity in a form which (a) avoids dissolution by historical relativity; (b) is coherent with Jesus; and (c) is not empty.

Humanist theology. Like many others, Hans Küng (*On Being a Christian*, 1974; Eng. trans. Collins 1977) thinks we live in a world now permanently non-religious and humanist. My concern for the purely religious, for salvation, and for the Transcendent is misguided. Christianity must be presented as the highest fulfilment of humanism.

It is only too true that the developed dogmatic faith was indeed the mother of humanism. But in modern humanist and liberal theology both God and Jesus tend to become mere symbolic reinforcements of a concern for the human in general. Does this not in the end approximate to Comtism—human self-infatuation tricked out in evocative religious metaphors?

The Primitive Faith. Eastertide is a coded liturgical monument to the primitive faith, and it is ended by the ascension. Luke and John believe the glory has departed. There is a clear distinction between a fortunate first generation who saw, and later generations who merely believe the apostolic faith. The apostles, we are told, lived in the presence and power of the *eschaton*, but the presence was withdrawn and subsequent generations perforce fell back into historical-dogmatic faith. We are told mythologically that the Lord was taken from their sight, but why the first immediacy had to be lost is not altogether clear.

99

Perhaps the ascension is itself the answer, for it stands for the beginning of a vast romantic elaboration of doctrine about Jesus which eventually almost drowned his voice.

Orthodoxy. We must distinguish between the elements of faith and the pattern in which they came to be arranged. I certainly make rather free with the orthodox pattern, but I keep more of the elements than might at first be thought.

The doctrine of the Trinity is an example. The elements are God the Father, Jesus the Son of God, and the divine Spirit. The pattern is the word Trinity, the co-equal triad clover-leaf doctrine of God, and the relatively modern distinction between upper- and lower-case, Son and son, Spirit and spirit.

The oldest images of the Trinity express the elements rather than the pattern—the baptism of Jesus, the crucifixion of Jesus, the Pentecostal gift of the Spirit. God's Spirit, God's communicated power of transcendence, first fills Jesus, and then through his work passes to his followers. Through Jesus men are united with God by God's Spirit. All that, we keep: the formula 'the Father, the Son and the Holy Spirit' sums up the Christian way to salvation.

But when 'the Trinity' was established as an eternal metaphysical Three in One and One in Three, a new image had to be coined to express the old truth. It was the assumption/coronation of the Virgin, in which the Three welcome a fourth. It was a preposterous image, but like so much of Marian doctrine it was needed to make good the losses sustained by the proclamation of Jesus' natural, co-eternal deity. It really is the case that, by setting aside the developed pattern, we may come to grasp the primitive elements better.

INDEX

Al-Hallaj   15f
Anselm   79f
Aristotle   95
Augustine of Hippo   46, 91
Austin, J. L.   95

Barth, K.   35
Basilides   85
Blakney, R. B.   51
Brunner, E.   47
Buddha, Buddhism   34, 70, 83
Bultmann, R.   48f, 54, 58, 72, 95, 98

Calvin, Calvinism   26, 46
Chadwick, H.   47
Charles, R. H.   98
Chillingworth, W.   26
Constantine   9, 83
Corbishley, T.   21
Crossan, J. D.   55

Eckhart   51
Eliot, George   23

Feuerbach, L.   95
Fichte, J. G.   95
Fuchs, E.   96

Hegel, G. E. F.   66, 95
Heidegger, M.   95
Hick, J. H.   90
Hinduism   34f, 70
Hodgson, P. C.   23

Ignatius of Antioch	19
Islam	34
Jeremias, J.	58, 60, 96f
Jüngel, E.	96
Kähler, M.	46
Kant, I.	29f, 45, 95
Kauffmann, W.	97
Kee, A.	98
Kierkegaard, S.	47f, 51, 66, 90f
Küng, H.	99
Lessing, G. E.	47, 49, 51
Linnemann, E.	96
Loëwe, H.	53
Luther, Lutheranism	9, 46, 96
Mahovee, M.	98
Maimonides, M.	95
Mansel, H. L.	93, 95
Marcion	86
Mill, J. S.	95
Moltmann, J.	98
Montefiore, C. G.	53
Mozart, W. A.	62
Mozley, E. N.	38
Nineham, D. E.	98
Paley, W.	95
Perrin, N.	49, 53, 55
Pius X	30
Plato	66
Ritschl, A.	44f, 56
Rubens, P. P.	97
Sanders, J. T.	40
Schleiermacher, F. D. E.	44
Schopenhauer, A.	90
Schweitzer, A.	27, 38f, 46, 98
Searle, J. R.	95

Socrates	58f, 66, 97
Stead, G. C.	85
Strauss, D. F.	22f, 95, 98
Thomas Aquinas	95
Troeltsch, E.	98
Weiss, J.	38f, 45f, 56, 98
Wilder, A. N.	96
Wittgenstein, L.	95